Human Character and Morality

———————◆———————

Human Character and Morality

Reflections from the History of Ideas

Stephen D. Hudson

Routledge & Kegan Paul
Boston, London and Henley

First published in 1986
by Routledge & Kegan Paul plc
9 Park Street, Boston, Mass. 02108, USA

14 Leicester Square, London WC2H 7PH, England and

Broadway House, Newtown Road,
Henley on Thames, Oxon RG9 1EN, England

Set in Imprint, 11 on 12pt
and printed in Great Britain
by Butler & Tanner Ltd, Frome and London

Library of Congress Cataloging in Publication Data

Hudson, Stephen D., 1950–
Human character and morality.

Bibliography: p.
Includes index.
1. Ethics.   2. Character.   I. Title.
BJ1012.H83   1986   170'.42   85–19291
British Library CIP data also available

ISBN 0–7102–0770–0

For Kee

Contents

Preface

———◆———

A gloomy, hair-brained enthusiast, after his death, may have a place in the calendar, but will scarcely ever be admitted when alive into intimacy and society, except by those as delirious and dismal as himself.

An Inquiry Concerning the Principles of Morals, 91–92

Philosophical questions often sound a touch absurd. Philosophers often are absurd. But people should not be too put off. That which represents the best – *philosophia perennis* – raises matters that press on each of us, consciously or unconsciously. Good philosophical thought shapes (and is shaped by) the way we think of ourselves. Hence it must have a practical effect on the quality of our lives.

Moral philosophy seems quintessentially philosophical, in the best sense of the philosophical tradition. It forges our thought, bending and hammering both how we think about ourselves and how we live. Human character responds to the pressure of moral thought. When we identify acts, or characters, or ways of life as shocking or disgraceful, repugnant, evil, despicable, or inhuman, dishonorable or wrong, we respond to that thought. Any moralist worth his salt recognizes this. Our behavior can be changed by changing our thought about it. This is a book that attempts to understand why moral philosophy – or, as I prefer to call it, moral theorizing – has this animating character. More specifically, the work attempts to understand the animating qualities of human character and moral thought and how they, together, place constraints on the adequacy of moral theories. This project is organized around a central contrast between two different philosophical conceptions of what morality is *about*. The great philosophical debates in moral theory do not occur within moral theory. They are, rather, about it: about its nature, structure, form. About the grounds for moral judgement, and not the judgement itself. About what justifies a practice, not what practices are justified. About the nature of moral reasons, not what moral reasons we have. As moral practitioners Hume and Kant were not very different. Their radical disagreement occurred up one level: at how one arrives at the practices, how morality engages us, where the grounds for our moral beliefs and attitudes lie, the relationship of God to the moral order.

I call the two different conceptions of what morality is about the 'Direct View' and the 'Indirect View.' Roughly, the Direct View holds that morality is primarily about *acts* or *conduct*: they are the primary moral phenomena, and the assessment of them is the primary moral task. Other moral phenomena – for example, moral agents and their traits, capacities, and motives – and their assessment are seen as secondary to or derivative from (assessments of) primary moral phenomena. The second conception, the Indirect View, denies the primacy of acts asserted by the Direct View; instead, it holds that moral agency and human character possess equal standing or are even more fundamental than acts. It is a version of the Indirect View that I defend.

My approach is not to argue straightforwardly for the superiority of a version of the Indirect View, but to build an argument through an extended exploration of the contrast between the two different conceptions. That contrast is to be had only through an understanding of how the moral thought of some of the major figures in the history of ethics is shaped by their advocacy of one of these views: for each of the conceptions is sufficiently rich that it can be embodied in strikingly different ways. Sidgwick, Kant, Hume and Aristotle are treated in some detail, though their theories are considered only in the light of this contrast; no attempt is made to sketch their overall theories.

It bears repeating that the contrast between the two differing conceptions cannot be adequately developed independently of the historical thought that informed and informs these conceptions. For, on the one hand, the conceptions are like an abstract building configuration – say, for example, a three story single family residence – that become philosophically interesting only when integrated with some set (or other) of architectural elements. And, on the other hand, our present ideas are tied to the historical conceptions that are revealed: they are reflections of them that shape and direct our thought.

My argument is, I fear, at times more complex and convoluted than many readers will like. I have no apologies for it, nonetheless. We are incredibly complex creatures and any discussion that attempts to reveal something about the core of our being and our thought must be a bit thick at times. It need not be obscure, though. Many of the deepest truths are quite simple. And we know them straight-away. But *understanding* them requires knowledge of how they fit together, what their interconnections are. Knowledge is often easily procured; understanding only rarely so.

Though I have no apologies for complexity where complexity is needed, I have no obscurantist sympathies. And since it should prove helpful to have a schematic outline of the project, what better opportunity than now?

In Chapter I an initial characterization of the distinction between the Direct and Indirect View is drawn. Since the latter conception is characterized as the denial of the former, it is important to heed that such a denial can take one of two forms. One, which I call the 'Strong Denial,' asserts that the assessment of moral agents and their character is the primary activity of morality; it, therefore, reverses the attribution, by the Direct View, of primacy to acts and second-class status to agents and their character. The other, which I call the 'Weak Denial,' maintains there is no primacy to be found for acts, nor for that matter, for agents.

I turn to Sidgwick in Chapter II. The purpose is to develop a more comprehensive and systematic understanding of the Direct View. It, like the Indirect View, is best explored through contrast with its sibling rival. Sidgwick is introduced as the first representative of the Direct View,

Aristotle of the Indirect. Each of these historical figures and their work is exploited to see how these two views connect with metaphysical and epistemological views to form a systematic whole.

Sidgwick's embrace of the Direct View is delineated through three theses he maintained. Since *any* version of the Direct (or Indirect) View will have a number of vital elements other than the keystone claim for the primacy of acts (or characters of agents), it is important to identify patterns of elements that fit well next to the keystone. For neither the Direct nor the Indirect View are evaluated in isolation, by themselves. They stand or fall, are modified or replaced, through scrutiny of their characteristic theoretical embodiment, or lacking that, in their various embodiments. This makes assessment of them a holistic assessment of the theoretical network in which they play a role; and, of course, makes the evaluation more complex and difficult. The best criticism shakes the whole tree; break off a limb and the criticism may find one of the earth's most sturdy creatures.

The vital element of Sidgwick's theory on which I focus is his rationalist conception of theoretical unity. I selected this since, on the one hand, it represents a dominant theme shared by many adherents of the Direct View, and, on the other, it does not fit easily into versions of the Indirect View. Hence it tells us something about each. A grasp of any complex position is enhanced by contrasting it with an opposing view. Aristotle's advocacy of the Indirect View is used, in Chapter IV, to provide such a set of contrastive highlights. However, before introducing this aspect of his moral thought, it is necessary to pave the way for a proper understanding of it by insuring that some common misapprehensions about the nature and role of moral virtues are eliminated. This I do in Chapter III. Specifically, I argue that accepted modern accounts of the role of virtues in moral theory – accounts that, if accurate, would prevent virtues from being a determinant of right action – are defective. Aristotle's theory of the virtues is not merely concerned with the good, but with a theory of the right and the good. The exact nature of the moral value of human excellences such as friendship and courage is a key to understanding both Hume's and Aristotle's contribution to the Indirect View. In Chapter III I describe this nature and attempt to explain why it has been misapprehended by others. I turn to the Aristotelian account to examine the detailed exemplification of such moral values in Chapter IV.

It emerges from the discussion in these early chapters that the modern notion of the rule of law plays an important role in informing most modern secular moral theories that are versions of the Direct View. One element of this notion is identified as the schema of act and motive. It was shared by any number of writers in the 18th and 19th centuries. In Chapter V I discuss several such writers, namely, Richard Price, Thomas Reid, and John Stuart Mill, to illustrate further details of the schema. And, to highlight its connection with accompanying metaphysical and epistemological theses. As always, securing a proper grasp of the differences between such views and versions of the Indirect View is the goal.

I turn to Hume in Chapter VI. The aim of this and the next several chapters is to reconstruct a sufficient portion of Hume's moral theory to reveal that his conception of human virtue is bifurcated; that each of the two different conceptions of human virtue rely decisively on a different conception of the moral point of view; that these different points of view are each moral points of view; that they are not reducible to some one moral point of view without moral loss, since they correctly characterize our moral situation. In pursuing this aim I hope that a deeper understanding of the Indirect View, and the relationship between moral principles and acts and agents, and their evaluations, will emerge. In particular, understanding Hume is crucial because his moral thought provides a particularly deep theoretical account of the *double* moral value that virtues such as friendship and generosity possess. Hence his theory of the interdependent nature of the right and the good, of which the double moral value of friendship is merely one reflection, merits the most serious attention. And not merely as a fascinating piece of history.

The discussion of Hume is quite lengthy. But deservedly

so, I think. If there is a sustained conception of our moral conceptions that exposes so much of both the Direct and the Indirect Views, and their (historically varying) religious, scientific, and metaphysical backdrops, it is to be found in Hume. If this were a novel, Hume would be the heroic protagonist. My intellectual debts to him are immense, and were enlarged even more in the course of this project.

Chapter VI merely functions as an expository introduction; it sets the stage and focus for the relevant portions of Hume's moral concerns. Chapters VII and VIII develop Hume's dualistic account of the virtues, exploring the rationale and implications of the account. Reduced to its simplest form, these chapters pursue the questions of why Hume's chronicle of our moral sensibilities, our moral consciousness, is to be regarded as lacking any singularity; and whether and why that makes it a better or worse account. Chapter IX reflects upon the Humean account; Chapter X upon what has gone before.

Some final comments on the text and its history. This work makes no claim to originality; rather, it claims to be unoriginal, in the best sense of the term. What I try to show throughout my argument is that the ideas about human character and morality that are central to understanding our moral situation are derived from reflections from the history of ideas. In addressing those ideas I have tried to characterize them accurately, giving them a sympathetic and properly historical rendering, without succumbing to the predilection for security that too often prevents serious students of history from *understanding* the implications of a system of ideas. I remain cognizant of the fact that the result is not beyond reasonable objection, that others might craft different emphases and discover connections that I have overlooked or (allegedly) misaligned. I encourage others to pursue such critical inquiries. I hope only that this work will aid such endeavors and will stand as one informative beacon in the history of ideas.

I sometimes argue strongly against an author's ideas. Such arguments, it should go without saying, are not a criticism of the author's intellect. Rather, it is the very depth and grandeur of his thought that makes it worthy of such attention. A systematic vision, even if flawed, is preferable to a well argued footnote. My sole wish is that my errors have a comparable scale.

Readers will quickly discover that there are several modern traditions about philosophical writing and inquiry that I do not share. First, philosophical inquiry is often presumed to be morally neutral. I do not share this presumption; indeed I think one cannot, and should not, be morally neutral. The image of philosophical inquiry as the paradigm of neutral and disinterested thought seems to me a false one: one which, if actually brought off, would be philosophically uninteresting.

Second, the modern tradition of philosophical writing is nonpolemical. Polemics, as found in editorials and politics, is, well, thought to have one foot in the cesspool of everyday debates: something seen somehow to be *beneath* philosophical inquiry. Such a division and elevation of philosophy from politics and everyday life is a modern cloak that, I suspect, will not persist.

Finally, in some circles of *academia* there is a popular idea that you can address the specialist or the nonspecialist, but not both. That if your writing is pedantic you are addressing the specialist and hence the pedantry is permitted; that if your writing is not pedantic, it's colloquial and therefore inappropriate for the specialist. This idea, it seems to me, reflects the unhealthy insular effects of self-serving academic circles. It is a pretentious idea whose historical roots undermine its apparent credibility.

One last editorial word. Analytic philosophy in the twentieth century has become a too small and self-contained circle. One too comforted by the myths of current wisdom; one which lacks a sense of historical perspective on itself; one whose chief vice is intellectual arrogance. This is a work in analytic philosophy and hence, no doubt, is afflicted by such maladies. I do hope it has escaped, to some extent. The degree to which it has not shows how one's roots doggedly pursue you, try what you will.

Parts of the material in Chapters III and IV spring from

earlier publication. I wish to thank the editors and publishers of *Ethics* and *The Australasian Journal of Philosophy* for permission to use this work.

The ideas expressed in this book have been shaped and reshaped, expanded and contracted, discarded and renewed over a period of years. During that time a number of people, whom I have had the good fortune to know, have had a considerable influence on their, and my, development. There are both special and general debts. A special debt is owed to Stephen Darwall, whose lengthy and insightful comments on an earlier draft of the manuscript improved it immeasurably. I am especially grateful to him since, as those who know him personally will realize, he is philosophically opposed to several of the key ideas presented here and is, nonetheless, one of the most fair-minded and generous critics to be found. Annette Baier's comments on an early draft of the three chapters on Hume's moral thought forced several important revisions. The final draft of the manuscript was completed while I was visiting the Philosophy Department at the University of Pennsylvania. To the members of the department and to the University of Pennsylvania I am grateful for the opportunity I was provided to complete this project in an atmosphere so congenial and hospitable to intellectual endeavors.

A number of philosophers have, in recent years, engaged in a sceptical inquiry about the nature of modern moral philosophy. Their work has left its indelible imprint on me and helped me to sustain this project through some difficult times. It therefore seems only appropriate that I should acknowledge this general intellectual debt to them and the paths they have paved. Here, I would include G. E. M. Anscombe, Philippa Foot, Bernard Williams, Myles Burnyeat, and Alasdair MacIntyre.

I am especially grateful to Annette Baier, Kurt Baier, John Cooper, Stephen Darwall, David Falk, and J. B. Schneewind, from each of whom I have learnt much about the nature of moral theory and the history of moral thought; each have, at various times, forced me to revise and rethink these and many other ideas. Their conversations, comments, and patient and unflagging interest in my work has

meant much more than I can express. The faults and deficiencies that remain are due to my somewhat contrary and
mulish nature, which these kind people tolerate so well.

Highland Park, N.J.   *Stephen D. Hudson*
December, 1984

I

What is Morality all About?

---◆---

We are discussing no trivial subject, but how a man should live.

Republic, 352D

How should we think about moral theorizing? What is its nature? Common sense and good reason informs us that moral theorizing is an attempt to articulate a systematic and informative set of answers to key moral questions. What are those questions? Well, some of the chief ones must be questions very like:

1 What makes some conduct right, some wrong? Some good, some bad? Some praiseworthy, some blameworthy?
2 What makes a person be a good person? A bad person? Praiseworthy? Blameworthy?
3 In what does the morally good life consist? How should a person live his life? What is the connection between a good life and a happy one?

These are not actually three questions, but three sorts of questions. They are the sorts of questions that any moral theory which pretends to be comprehensive must address. Hence, in one form or another they will recur throughout this work, which takes as its focus how these questions must be addressed by an adequate moral theory.

Each of the sorts of questions reminds us that judgement and evaluation are essential activities of moral beings. What the questions organize are the things (or types of things) that are the objects of moral judgements. In the first case

1

that which is evaluated is actions or kinds of actions, in the second it is persons, in the third it is types of lives. What are the connections between the answers to these questions? For instance, can a person be morally good even when he performs acts that are morally wrong? Can an evil person lead a happy life, a good person an unhappy one?

Moral theorizing must answer such questions. Moral philosophy must address the question 'How should one live?,' understood in its most comprehensive sense. The chief and principal point of engaging in practical reasoning, of bothering to deliberate about practical matters at all, is the improvement of human life. Moral reasoning must have this goal as a distant and abstract target, or it is not practical reasoning. It has therefore seemed natural to think of moral theory as an attempt to formulate general principles of conduct that will provide a satisfactory answer to the question of how one should live. The crux of this idea is that if we can but answer the first question – to wit, in what conduct should one engage, from what conduct should one refrain – then answers to all further moral questions will fall into place, if we entertain them with sufficient ingenuity.

On reflection, it is clear that even a so simple and extraordinarily vague statement about the nature of our moral enterprise embodies a meta-theoretical perspective on the nature of moral theorizing: as with all thought, a conception of the nature of the project partially guides the direction of the undertaking. Let's try to expose the details of this perspective.

For ease of reference, let's begin by giving the perspective a name. Call it the 'Direct View.' What is the character of the Direct View? Simply put, the Direct View takes the moral evaluation of acts to have an ineliminable primacy; it takes the question 'What act should be performed?' as the most fundamental question a moralist can raise. In other words, questions of the first sort (in our list above) are taken as basic. All sorts of questions are derivative.

What exactly is meant by saying that the moral evaluation of acts is primary and what other moral evaluations are secondary or derivative? Roughly, that moral theory should (and must) first assign correct evaluations to acts (or kinds of acts). For instance, suppose that appraisals of acts were to be made in terms of moral rightness or wrongness; the requirement would then state that the primary task of moral theory is to elucidate the standards by which acts are correctly assigned their rating: being right, wrong, or neither. Moral theory cannot proceed to address other moral questions on a sound footing until its primary function has been executed. Why? Because the answer to these further questions presupposes that the prior questions about the moral character of acts have been resolved. Why? Because we cannot uncover answers to these other moral questions unless we already know what acts are right or wrong. How could you possibly know that a person was morally good, was praiseworthy, was living a life that did not conflict with morality, unless you could recognize the moral character of his acts?

The Direct View is a commonplace, even though it maintains several theses that are subject to dispute. Indeed, it is such a commonplace that many people accept it as the only plausible description of the nature of moral theorizing (and hence moral theory). For instance, Alan Donagan, in his *The Theory of Morality*, takes his primary task as a moral theorist to be one of locating that part of common morality that forms a correct moral system.[1] Common morality is characterized as a system of precepts about the moral permissibility of human actions, considered objectively. Thus Donagan takes the task of the moral theorist to be the development of a principled method for sorting the precepts of common morality by separating the correct ones from the incorrect ones. And, given his characterization of common morality, he thereby becomes an advocate of the Direct View. To be sure, Donagan recognizes that a 'moral system which confines itself to laying down what kinds of action, objectively considered, are permissible or not' would be 'incomplete.'[2] A complete moral system also addresses questions about the spirit in which a person acts. But such questions are secondary; they make no sense whatsoever except against the background of an assessment of actions themselves as permissible or impermissible.[3]

The Direct View is orthodox. That makes it even more surprising that a good number of classical moral philosophers are not advocates. How can it be that thinkers of the stature of Kant, Hume, and Aristotle oppose the Direct View and yet hardly anyone takes notice? The answer, I think, lies in the emergence and acceptance of a new tradition – the modern notion of the rule of law and the sort of liberalism that underlies both the social contract tradition and utilitarianism – and, most importantly, the implicit ideals of theoretical unity and completeness, of moral perfection and the powers of reason, found within the eddies of the new current. By the end of the 19th century *our* moral consciousness had been shaped and informed by this new player to the extent that the Direct View became, and remains, an authoritative expression of pre-reflective morality. Kant and Hume, and Aristotle, to a lesser extent, are read in this light: to reveal what they can contribute to the completion of the moral project (as conceived by the Direct View). The implicit disagreement, due to these writers' advocacy of the Indirect View, is often hidden because both sides focus on how actions are assessed (to enable us to understand how we should live). So what differences occur are often unnoticed, or swept aside, or regarded as merely verbal. But they should not be. For the differences carry critical thought about morality pretty deep.

Let's introduce a second perspective on the nature of moral theorizing: the 'Indirect View.' Later we shall want to look at the details of how it is advanced by some of its advocates – Kant, Hume, and Aristotle – in greater depth; at present, though, we merely want to formulate an initial statement of the position. Roughly, then, how should we characterize the Indirect View?

Consider, again, how we have initially characterized the Direct View. Concerned primarily with the assessment of acts or kinds of acts, it conceives the task of moral theory to be the elucidation of the standards by which choice should be guided; if you like, we can say that it always has a certain picture in mind of what we look like when we confront moral problems. We are faced with choosing between various alternative courses of action. Should we sign up for the draft? Should we ignore the law that requires this? Should we openly defy it? Should we move to Canada?

The most fundamental task of moral theory is said to be the elucidation of how we are to answer such questions. In this sense the Direct View takes the question 'What ought I to do?' to be the most fundamental moral question. It envisages this question to be raised, again, again, and again, in situations of choice throughout one's life. And the sum of the occurrences of such questions – with, of course, the correct answers – represents how moral theory answers the question 'How should one live?'[4] A systematic set of principles that organizes these answers – what is commonly called the principles or standards of morality – is what moral theory is supposed to uncover, to establish. That's what moral theory, and morality, are all about.

The Indirect View does not deny that the question 'What ought I to do?' is a key moral question. Nor even that it is a fundamental one. Only that it is *the* fundamental question of morality. In making this denial the Indirect View does not assert that the question 'How should one live?' fails to provide the point for engagement in moral reflection. It only denies that the relationship between this question and its answer is straightforward, as the Direct View maintains. The Indirect View holds that one cannot simply go *forthwith* to the principles of conduct that sort acts (or types of acts) into classifications (such as 'morally acceptable' and 'morally unacceptable'). This avenue is not actually accessible. Instead, the moral theorist must pursue a somewhat circuitous path to arrive at such principles; he must first engage in a somewhat detailed examination of the nature of *moral agency*, in order to be in a position to answer questions of the sort that the Direct View takes as basic and fundamental.

The manner in which we have just characterized the Indirect View, though something of an advance, needs much improvement. In particular, our present characterization suffers from a serious ambiguity. The Direct View takes as an obvious truism that acts have primacy, that the virtue of acts is the concern of morality, and that moral theorizing reflects this concern by developing procedures for segregating virtuous acts from others. The denial of the Direct View, then, could take either of two forms. First, it could assert the primacy of agents. So understood, the Indirect

View would provide the mirror image of the Direct: while the Direct asserts the primacy of acts and grants the virtue of agents only a secondary and derivative role, the Indirect would assert the primacy of agents and grant the virtue of acts only a secondary and derivative role. The second interpretation, on the other hand, would not be so radical. If the Direct View claims that the question 'What ought I to do?' must be answered prior to and independently from the question 'What sort of person ought I to be?,' the second form of the Indirect View would not reverse the priorities. It would maintain that Direct View goes astray because there are no priorities here of the kind asserted; the answers to these two questions are *interdependent*, and hence principles about the virtue of agents play the same indispensable role in answering questions about the conduct of one's life that principles about the virtue of acts do. The traffic on the road of virtue from acts to agents flows in both directions, from no particular starting point, with no set terminus.

Let's call the first form the 'Strong Denial,' and the second the 'Weak Denial,' whenever we need to distinguish between the two forms. As we shall see, Kant and Martineau propose versions of the Strong Denial,[5] while Hume and Aristotle support the Weak Denial. There are, of course, many other variations and meanderings within the parameters of both the Direct and Indirect Views. The history of moral thought is rich and subtle; and since these two perspectives are aspects of complex systems of thought, the student of that history will encounter many different ways in which these horizons are enriched and informed by other facets of a system of ideas to which they are connected.

In fact, it is most likely best not to proceed with any further clarification of the Direct and Indirect Views *in abstracto*; all ideas have historical roots from which one can venture only so far without loss of understanding. We should turn to an historical example of advocacy of one of the Views to enrich our sense of them. Bear in mind that the purpose of the examination is not to arrive at the final, definitive statement of the character of the Direct and Indirect Views; it is, rather, to provide a better understanding of their core. No final characterization will be derived, though, because there is none. The history of these ideas is not yet finished; further exploration and testing of their limits and significance is yet to come.

The Direct and Indirect Views are descriptions of philosophical perspectives on the nature of morality. As with all philosophical perspectives, one is initially attracted because one shares the metaphysical assumptions and social conventions that supply the roots to nourish the perspective. When you or I come to think about the nature of morality, we do not initiate our examination from the thoroughgoing (and balmy) point of view of a *tabula rasa*. We carry some mental baggage with us. Always. We have families of beliefs about the world and its nature, including beliefs about, say, us, morality, and rationality. Conceptions of the natural world, humanity, God, and human and moral perfection: these are but a few of the hidden winds that spread the sails of our reflective comprehension of ourselves and our social order. If we call such beliefs 'first-order beliefs,' it is immediately apparent that our mental luggage carries other sorts of apparel as well. We also have what we might call 'second-order beliefs:' for example, beliefs about how we should talk about, say, morality, what the objects of our first-order beliefs should be, and what sorts of things are appropriate to attribute to such objects. That is to say, the predicates we employ in moral propositions (to express our first-order moral beliefs) and the concepts by which we select their subjects are rooted in metaphysical propositions and social conventions that secure a general moral viewpoint. And we begin our examination from within such a viewpoint. Always.

The interconnections between our beliefs, viewpoints or outlooks, and critical thought is, to be sure, not unique to morality or moral thought; these same complex interconnections and relations make knowledge and critical investigation possible, whether, say, the knowledge is moral knowledge, scientific, or some other sort.

To return to the primary focus of business. Let's now inquire further into the nature of the Direct View by seeing how Sidgwick's moral theorizing is wedded to it.

II

Sidgwick: The Direct View

———————◆———————

The good of any one individual is of no more importance, from
the point of view (if I may say so) of the Universe, than the
good of any other.

The Methods of Ethics, 322

Since it is certainly true that under *both* the Direct and
Indirect views we can find a wide variety of logically independent views in a straightforward sense – namely, that a
view is Direct (or Indirect) does not dictate any particular
moral principle (e.g., the principle of utility, the golden
rule) will be recognized as sound or fundamental – substan-
tively different and incompatible moral theories will each
be instances of the Direct View and the Indirect View.
What makes a theory Direct or Indirect is located in its
conception of what morality is *about*. In this sense an examination of these two different views is a metamoral one.
That it is metamoral, however, does not imply that it lacks
moral import, that it is morally neutral between possible
theories. For as we will plainly see, whether one holds a
Direct or Indirect view has very substantial effects on what
sort of moral theory one will be inclined to see as plausible.

Given that the Direct View can be embodied in a number
of different moral theories – that it can be found in an
intuitionist's theory, or a utilitarian's or a modern Kantian's
– the question naturally arises as to why Sidgwick is chosen
as the first exemplar of the theory. Why indeed?

Several considerations are relevant. First, there is a historical consideration. The emergence and acceptance of a
new tradition – the modern notion of the rule of law and
the sort of liberalism that underlies both the social contract

tradition and utilitarianism – funds the common acceptance of the Direct View as obvious, as an expression of pre-reflective morality. But that tradition's growth was spurred by the acceptance of certain ideals of theoretical unity and completeness, of moral perfection and the powers of reason. And Sidgwick's thought represents several of these themes well. In this way his thought provides an insightful look at several underlying themes that tend, I think, to make, or have made, the Direct View attractive: that moral judgements, being about acts and the values they possess, are rationally justifiable because there is a rational procedure for the assignment of such values. Though not every advocate of the Direct View will agree with Sidgwick about the nature of the procedure he specifies, or his conception of practical rationality, or the relationship between reason and moral judgement, most will, I think, find the Direct Views attractive for reasons that are comparable, in kind, to the ones Sidgwick displays. Second, I wish, eventually, to engage in a Humean project: to purge the rationalist bent from the Direct View to see what attractions it then holds. Sidgwick represents that rationalist bent as well as any one.

Sidgwick's embrace of the Direct View is a portrait of the complex fabric of interconnections found in systematic thought. Let's focus on some aspects of the grid to elucidate the nature of the Direct View. Bear in mind that we shall risk oversimplifying matters a bit in order to crystallize some of the attractions the Direct View seems to hold.[1]

Sidgwick is committed to three propositions, or better, theses, which together entail (but are not entailed by) the Direct View. What are they?

First, and perhaps most simply, he takes the most elementary subject for moral predicates to be actions. He takes moral judgements to express propositions that attribute certain qualities to their subjects; the sort of subject to which these qualities are attributed is an action. He concurs with the Direct View's insistence that the primary subject of moral judgements is acts or kinds of acts, if only because he concurs that the subject is conduct.

Second, Sidgwick holds certain moral values to be fundamental. This second thesis is given a linguistic presentation:

9

certain predicates, namely, 'right,' 'wrong,' 'duty,' and 'ought,' are claimed to be primary. Combining these first two theses, then, we see that he takes fundamental moral judgements to take one of the following forms:

1 This act is right (wrong, neither).
2 It is (not) a duty to (fail to) perform this action.
3 This action ought (not) to be performed.

Moreover, he holds that these apparently different forms are not really different at all. For the terms 'right,' 'wrong,' 'duty,' and 'ought' are held to be interdefinable. They express an elementary notion – the demands of reason on action – that is itself simple and undefinable.[2] For our present purposes Sidgwick's intuitionist objections to reductionist definitions of moral terms, objections that were repeated and made famous by G. E. Moore in the 20th century, are unimportant. As are his particular choices of the moral predicates chosen for the privileged position of most elementary. There are no *a priori* reasons why an advocate of the Direct View could not select a different set of elementary predicates: say, for example, 'morally good,' and 'worthy of moral approval.' Nor does the Direct View itself conflict with a reductionist account of moral terms; it is compatible with so-called 'Naturalistic' definitions – such as, for example, that 'right' means 'will be approved by knowledgeable people familiar with the facts of the case' – whether they take a reductionist or a nonreductionist form.

The third thesis that delineates Sidgwick's embrace of the Direct View is related, *in his thought*, to these matters. His version of the Direct View is informed by his understanding of the nature of moral rightness and duty: an understanding that is greatly influenced by Kant. Put most simply, his view is that 'right' and 'duty' and 'ought' matters. His version of the Direct View is informed by his understanding of the nature of moral rightness and duty: an understanding that is greatly influenced by Kant. Put most simply, his view is that 'right' and 'duty' and 'ought' express the demands of practical reason and action. Moral judgements that employ these predicates provide sound directives for action if and only if the propositions they express are dictated by practical rationality. Moral thought relies essentially upon some conception of practical reasoning; that conception must be employed in providing the account of how the most elementary moral predicates are to be applied correctly to their subjects.

It is Sidgwick's conception of practical rationality, therefore, that leads to the third thesis. We can express that thesis, in a somewhat technical form, by saying that it requires all sound moral principles to be functions. Any such function would have as its domain the set of situations in which a person might find himself; its values would be the acts assigned to the arguments as being right or wrong.

Let's express the thesis in a non-technical manner. A function is a rule that applies to something – its arguments – and yields a result – its value. Consider the operation of taking the absolute value of a number. This operation changes a negative number into a corresponding positive number, leaving the value of the positive number unchanged. The absolute value of '-3,' for example, is '3,' and the absolute value of '8' is '8.' Let 'ABS' represent the absolute value function. To represent the computation of the absolute value of '-6' we write:

$$ABS(-6) = 6$$

The numbers placed inside the parentheses – in the present case, we find '-6' – are the arguments of the function; they are the things to which the function or rule is applied. The numbers that occur to the right of the equal sign are the values of the function; they are the results of the application of the function to some argument. A function just is an assignment of values to arguments. And the set of all arguments to which the function assigns values is the domain of the function.

Sidgwick's third thesis cements the alliance between the first two. It prescribes how the fundamental subjects of moral judgements get associated with the correct fundamental moral predicates: through a rule or a function. Suppose you are in some situation, call it S_1, and are attempting to decide what it is that you ought to do. Sidgwick's view is that for *any* such situation, S_n, there is a moral judgement that correctly tells you what to do because it is an expression of the function that assigns to every act (that can be performed in any such situation) the correct value. If we let 'A_{1-n}' represent the various acts that are candidates for choice, and 'MORAL' represent a moral function of the sort that backs moral judgements, we can represent the idea roughly by:

$$MORAL(S_1) = A_1 \text{ is wrong to fail to do}$$

Such is Sidgwick's idea. It is astonishing. Morality is held to be fully determinate: all acts fall within the scope of its appraisals are assigned values and the assignment eliminates all moral conflict. The problem of moral conflict is spurious, merely an apparent problem that can be shown, *a priori*, to be nonexistent. Let's explore this matter further.

The third thesis is a result of Sidgwick's conception of practical rationality and his claim that moral propositions express the demands of reason on action. Morality is taken to represent the fullest expression of rational nature, and as such, must be completely rationalized. Hence any moral theory that fails to satisfy the canons of fullest rationality will be rejected as inadequate. What we find here, then, is a conception of theoretical unity, a model of a *perfect* moral theory, generated by the association of moral theories with a model of rational nature. And what exactly is it that makes a moral theory perfect? If we reconstruct the argument that yields Sidgwick's third thesis as its conclusion, we see a theory is perfected when it becomes *complete* and *unitary*. Let's fashion that argument.

Rationality requires consistency. A set of normative principles, such as moral principles, are supposed to provide reasons for acting. Hence the set must be consistent. And it will be consistent if and only if it applies without conflict to all cases. Why?

Well, the principle is supposed to provide reasons for acting. It does so through its role as the major premise of a practical syllogism. The justificatory force of a practical argument (allegedly) lies primarily in the major premise: the premise which, when applied to the facts of the case (as stated in the minor premise), entails the conclusion: a directive that states what action is (not) to be performed. Suppose that conflicting prescriptions were entailed. That is, suppose that one directive told you to perform some act, call it A_x, another directive told you to perform some act A_y, and you could not perform both. It cannot be the case that reason dictates that you should perform both. Hence, the principles used as major premises in practical arguments cannot generate such conflict. Or, more precisely, they cannot conflict in any ineliminable manner. For if principle R entails that A_x is to be done and principle S entails that A_y is to be done, *but* one principle, say R, always takes precedence in such situations, then the conflict is not worrisome. (It is not even conflict, is it?)

It is an all too familiar fact – one with which Sidgwick was preoccupied – that if there is a multiplicity of moral principles, they are liable to come into conflict at times. Yet from the perspective of our everyday moral thinking and practice, it is transparent that we continually invoke different moral principles to justify our conduct. I meet you because I promised. It goes without saying – save by moral philosophers – that promises ought to be kept. I fail to keep my promise because there is a medical emergency in my family that requires my attention. Of course, I ought to take my brother to the hospital, even if I shall be rather late for our meeting. Such prosaic examples that assert the soundness of received wisdom troubled Sidgwick. For if there is a multiplicity of moral principles used to justify conduct and they, at times, come into conflict in particular cases, then the prescriptions they entail will at those times be inconsistent. Hence they cannot express the demands of reason on action.

What is needed is some method for resolving such conflicts. Without it – whether it is a supreme principle that decides all conflicts, say, in the way that a referee has the final say in many games, or a system of priority rules that orders all principles, telling us which ones take precedence when, or elaborate exceptive clauses attached to each principle so that all conflicts are eliminated – practical reasoning results in inconsistencies.

Since practical reason is not inconsistent, sound moral principles must have the character attributed to them in the third thesis: they must be functions or rules that apply to every situation in which a person might find himself and determine the most reasonable thing to do in that situation. As Sidgwick himself puts it,

> general rules and maxims may in their turn be found mutually inconsistent, in either sense; and here too conduct appears to us irrational or at least imperfectly irrational, not only if the maxims upon which it is professedly based conflict with and contradict one another, but also if they cannot be bound together by means of some fundamental principle. For practical reason does not seem to be thoroughly realised until *perfect order*, *harmony*, and *unity of system* is introduced in all our actions.[3]

As a moral theorist one should quarrel with Sidgwick's rationalist bent on any number of grounds. Two of the more pressing issues – each of which are treated by him in a seriously inadequate manner – are the conception of the ideal of practical rationality and the characterization of practical reasoning as deductive or defective. The latter is patently false; the former is deeply troubling. For Sidgwick is correct in thinking that moral theorizing presupposes and utilizes in an essential way some conception of the nature of practical rationality. But he merely takes for granted the orthodox rationalist dogma that rationality is unitary, that all practical truths that yield solutions to our moral and political problems form a harmonious system in which all solutions are fully compatible and commensurable. A moral problem for which there is no solution *must* be counterfeit: the function of reason is to solve, to surmount the force of circumstances, to triumph over nature. We find two philosophical dogmas here: the metaphysics of the monistic rationalists, that all truly good things are part of a single, perfect whole, and *a priori* optimism about the power of reason.

Were it but so. Reality is recalcitrant and has thus far refused to conform to the rationalists' conception. The stronger case seems to be made for the other side: that conflict is essential to rational life, not incompatible with it. The rational life is the life of creatures like ourselves, who need to employ reason because the demands of our complex nature are manifold and not always harmonious. Practical intelligence has evolved because it solves problems and meets demands created by our emotional needs and temperament; but it also creates new demands and needs. (Everything has its price.) Our life is like raising a child: it consists of a wide set of activities (like, for example, disciplining the child, playing, conversing, teaching and learning) that exhibit many interests and concerns that come into conflict and must be addressed, balanced, modified, reviewed, tried one way and then another. That is the nature of human life as we know and experience it; it is not a unitary enterprise.

Sidgwick thought otherwise. Our moral life, taken as the highest expression of rationality, was thought to possess 'perfect order, harmony, and unity of system,' insofar as it embodies a thoroughly adequate method of ethics. Why should we disagree? Where does the case against such rationalism lie?

Initially, it is found in our moral experience. We experience moral conflict; we find ourselves, at times, in situations where our considered judgement is that there are two different acts, each of which ought to be performed, but both of which cannot. Such situations can present serious dilemmas – as when we can save the life of only one of the two persons trapped in a fiery automobile – or choices which, though not as painful and for which no grounds for preference exist, are the cause for sincere regret nonetheless. A promise that should be broken because some other act is morally best does not thereby have no moral force.[4] That we should regret having broken our promise, that in some cases we owe compensation even though our conduct was morally justified, these facts speak against the rationalist.

To what extent can we be confident that there *must* be some morally best thing to do, always? To what extent does practical reason dictate that, wherever moral appraisals are appropriate, there must be a morally determinate, conflict-free outcome? Rationalists maintain no moral conflicts are genuine, and that morality is fully determinate. But what are the grounds for their confidence? How do they know *a priori* that a satisfactory moral theory must *guarantee determinacy* and *harmony* in all cases? One can, of course, hope such a theory will be discovered. But isn't it an *empirical* matter whether all cases are determinate? Whether moral conflict will disappear or persist?

Bernard Williams[5] has located a key principle that governs many people's appreciation of moral conflicts. To see what role it plays in our moral understanding consider a situation where such conflicts occur. If we let '*a*' and '*b*' represent different acts, that situation seems aptly described by three statements:

(1)   A person, K, ought to perform act *a*.
(2)   K ought to perform *b*.
(3)   K cannot both perform *a* and perform *b*.

As Williams remarks, any three such claims do not form an inconsistent set; hence a moral theory that generates such a triad need not be faulty because it leads to contradictions. There is an inconsistency, however, if two principles are imported. One is some version of the familiar 'ought' implies 'can' principle: for any act which one truly ought to perform, it must be the case that one can perform. The second, which is the one on which we will focus, is what Williams calls the 'agglomeration principle:' it states, roughly, that a rule of conjunctive inference for statements like (1) and (2) is sound. That is to say, the agglomeration principle licenses the inference from the truth that you ought to help your parent and the truth that you ought to fight for your country, to the truth that you ought both to help your parent and fight for your country.

Now people often treat statements like (1)–(3) as inconsistent; and it is clear that such treatment is warranted if each of these additional principles are accepted as well. For employing the agglomeration principle on (1) and (2) yields:

(4)   K ought both to perform *a* and to perform *b*.

Which, when used with the principle that 'ought' implies 'can,' leaves one with:

(5)   K can perform both *a* and *b*.

So something must be forsaken to avoid the inconsistency. There are three obvious candidates: the 'ought' implies 'can' principle, the agglomeration principle, or that there

16

are no genuine moral conflicts since any three statements like (1)–(3) cannot all be true at the same time. Williams suggests that if we employ the agglomeration principle in moral reasoning, we shouldn't. For, as he puts it, the fact that in these situations of moral conflict we have due cause for regret, no matter what we do, shows that the last option falsifies our moral experience.[6]

Williams also observes that the agglomeration principle falters in other areas; it does not, for instance, hold for what is desirable, or prudent, or advisable. And this is a matter that warrants further study. For it holds the prospect, I think, of *explaining* why the agglomeration principle does not express the nature of practical reasoning. And hence why it should not be employed in moral reasoning.

Start with two things that are desirable. You've just had dinner. Eating a piece of cake is something that is now desirable. Eating a cup of ice cream is something that is now desirable. But you do not infer that eating both the piece of cake and the cup of ice cream is desirable. And you should not. For whether eating both is desirable is not an assessment that is settled by the prior individual appraisal of each.

Judgements of prudence share this feature. Suppose it is prudent to buy a car now. Inflation is on the rage, prices are rising, and you have access to a relatively decent loan rate. These same considerations may support the judgement that it is prudent to buy a house now. Suppose they do. It is imprudent to infer that prudence counsels you to buy both. What's more, buying both could be imprudent: as, for example, when the joint purchase would overextend you.

What is the moral of these two examples? Simply that judgements of reasonableness and desirability do not agglomerate. And it is relatively clear why they do not. Consider the general case, which we might represent as:

(1) It is reasonable to do x.
(2) It is reasonable to do y.

Suppose (1) and (2) are true. They do not guarantee the truth of

(3) It is reasonable both to do x and y.

The failure of agglomeration is due to the manner in which the reasonableness of individual lines of conduct are appraised. The first course of action is assessed in relation to what's reasonable for the agent to do in the circumstance he finds himself. Call the features of that situation 'C_1.' That set of features is exactly the set of features in relation to which the second line of conduct is appraised. But, now, assuming that x and y are distinct actions, the appraisal of performing *both* x and y must be made in relation to a set of circumstances *not identical* to C_1. Why? Simply because the appraisal of the reasonableness of performing both acts requires imagining what C_1 will be like after x is pursued and *then* asking whether, *in those altered circumstances*, y is to be pursued (or imagining what C_1 will be like after y is pursued and then asking whether, in those altered circumstances, x is to be pursued). It is this transformation of the circumstances that prevents agglomeration from being truth preserving.

We can summarize this result in a somewhat different fashion by insisting that judgements of reasonableness are relational judgements, and that, hence, (1) and (2) are best represented as:

(4)   It is reasonable, in C_1, to do x.
(5)   It is reasonable, in C_1, to do y.

And (3) is best represented as

(3)   It is reasonable, in C_1, both to do x and to do y.

But the agglomeration principle can now be seen to misconstrue the nature of practical rationality. For it makes it appear that one can reasonably assess performing both actions without appraising one of the pair in some set of circumstances that represents how C_1 would be altered by the performance of the other member of the pair. Hence it falsifies the nature of practical rationality.[7] But if the agglomeration principle does not work here, we have no reason to believe that it will work for moral judgements, which are merely one species of judgements of practical rationality.

Further reflection on these considerations about the appraisal of pairs of actions reminds us that the *coordination* of different actions of the same person, or *of different people*, plays a fundamental role in their evaluations. The role of coordination suggests a second problem for Sidgwick's view that an adequate moral theory must introduce perfect order, harmony and unity into our moral practices. Recall that Sidgwick's implementation of the Direct View is structured by a conception of theoretical unity and completeness: what it is like to develop an adequate theoretical representation for what morality is all about. That model required that all acts subject to evaluation be assigned a moral value (permissible, obligatory, impermissible), that no assignments could conflict, and that each of acts assigned the value of being obligatory can be implemented in practice by the person to whom it is assigned.

Question: Can we realistically expect all acts subject to moral evaluation to be coordinated in this manner? I think not. Let's attempt to muster some of the considerations that support this assessment.[8]

Suppose, for purposes of argument, that we have a set of moral precepts or general principles that, when applied to all cases subject to moral evaluation, allegedly satisfy Sidgwick's requirements. The set of actions assigned moral values must not merely be a consistent set, but must also be consistent with a 'Personal Ability Requirement': a moral principle that is some version of an 'ought' implies 'can' principle. Let's suppose that the Personal Ability Requirement reads: 'an act can be one that a person ought to perform (or is obligatory to perform) if and only if the person can perform that act.' Certain acts, for instance, that I am (presently) under an obligation to meet you yesterday, are inconsistent with the Personal Ability Requirement. Thus the Personal Ability Requirement is a condition that partially specifies a conception of completeness by supplementing the notion of *logical* inconsistency that also plays such a role.

A theory that violated the Personal Ability Requirement would thwart itself. Why? One of the chief objectives of moral theory is to provide guidance to persons, to direct them to choose the acts that are appropriate in the context of deliberation. The precepts of a theory that informed a person to perform acts that could not be performed would fail to achieve this objective. And hence would be a self-defeating theory. But reflection upon this objective of action guidance reveals that the Personal Ability Requirement must be seen as merely one side of a coin upon which one also finds a 'Coordination Requirement.' A theory that violated the Personal Ability Requirement would be one that generated directives with which at least one person could not comply (because some directives fail to satisfy Personal Ability Requirement). But a theory could be satisfactory on this score, but a disaster on another: it could issue directives with which (at least) two people could not jointly comply. That is, the theory could fail to *coordinate* the actions of the *different* persons to whom it applies, thereby preventing the directed conduct of one person from competing with the directed conduct of another. Consider a simple example. Suppose the theory tells us that Jones has a duty to take several wives and have many children, while it tells Smith that she has a duty to prevent polygamy. The situation, roughly, would be that Jones has a duty to prevent Smith from doing her duty, just as Smith has a duty to prevent Jones from doing his. Hence, even though each could perform their duty if the other did not, they could not each succeed in performing their duty. Call any such situation a failure of 'design coordination:' it represents a failure on the part of the theory like that of the building contractor who orders extra help on Tuesday to pour the foundation, but asks for delivery of the cement on Monday. The Coordination Requirement, then, is simply that there be no failures of design coordination. For such failures signify that the theory's objective of action guidance has not been satisfied for all agents to whom it is addressed.

What is necessary to avoid a failure of design coordination? The first intuition of many is that the set of moral precepts that forms the body of the theory must generate directives that can be successfully executed by the person(s) to whom they apply: that is, each and every directive that is generated by the theory (telling people what to do in the various circumstances they find themselves through life) is not merely something that the person to whom it applies can do, but is something which, if done, will not, for that very reason, prevent anyone else from doing that which they are directed to do.

It takes not much reflection to see that this requirement is most difficult to achieve in practice. (To say that the requirement is satisfied in theory, in an ideal, is empty: the difficulty of satisfying the requirement is due to the complexity of achieving design coordination in the world; it is a Pyrrhic victory to overcome the difficulty by eliminating it.) We have limited knowledge of the causal principles that govern the world; we have limited knowledge of our circumstances, in the sense of knowledge of the total course of events that constitutes our world and how these events relate to our present action; we have limited powers to implement changes we believe are warranted or desirable. Each of these factors seriously impedes design coordination.

Some other practical matters can perhaps serve as useful bases for reminding us of the degree of difficulty in satisfying the coordination requirement. Suppose, *arguendo*, that we in our moral affairs are like economists with respect to economic affairs. We agree that a reduction in the federal deficit is a desirable objective. But how is it to be brought about without serious disruption, harm, or injury to our economy? To ourselves? Will raising corporate taxes actually be counterproductive, since (as it is alleged) it will quell capital investment and increased hiring (which in turn reduces government expenditures in terms of unemployment support and increases revenues through increased payroll taxes)? Or will increasing corporate taxes reduce the deficit, which in turn will reduce interest rates and lead to a healthy and robust economy? Or, again, imagine yourself to be the coach of a professional football team. Your goal is to satisfy the coordination requirement for members of your team; that's the way to win. Why is it that you cannot produce a set of rules that tells each individual player what is the best action to perform in any situation that he faces?

The matter is even more complicated, is it not? Design coordination is thorny in even such a relatively simple case like football because it is affected not merely by limitations of knowledge and powers to bring about change, but also because the world is no idyllic collaborator. It rains and snows; this field is a muck; your player slips; another forgets his assignment. These facts about the way the world is are, often enough, ignored by the elegant designs of theorists. Precepts and maxims are characteristically tested, if only in the imagination, under a particular assumption of *agent ideality*: that the persons to whom they apply want to follow their directives, will, and will not make mistakes or have accidents, and so forth. But in practice we are not agents who possess these ideal characteristics, and hence what co-ordination obtains under the assumption of agent ideality can easily be lost in practice. There are at least two particularly pressing problems here, each of which pertains to conflicts that arise from people's failure to satisfy the directives of a moral theory. First, how should a theory instruct those persons who, because they have already violated some directive, can no longer obey all directives that apply to them (when they could have obeyed every directive if they had previously violated none)? And, second how should the theory address those persons who, though they have not violated some directive, can no longer obey all directives that apply to them because some other persons have violated some directive(s)?

Alan Donagan, in his recent attempt to show that a rationalist moral theory can be complete because no *genuine* cases of conflicts of duties arise,[9] provides a partial answer. Any genuine case of conflicting duties would entail that not all the precepts of the rationalist's moral system are obeyable. But Donagan, borrowing from Aquinas, calls to our attention that conflicts of duty that arise out of violations of duty should not count as genuine conflicts of duty that *undermine* the system of principles. After all, the fact that someone violates a precept and subsequently is unable to satisfy a precept (unless he disobeys another) hardly seems to show an inconsistency *in the system* of precepts. Following Aquinas, Donagan calls any *such* conflict of duties, where a person faces perplexity because he has previously disobeyed a moral precept, perplexity *secundum quid*. A moral system that permits such conflicts, Donagan notes, possesses no inconsistency or flaw. (Presumably, it recognizes that human nature being what it is, no system of moral precepts will prevent moral conflicts among the wicked.) But, there is a second sort of perplexity or conflict of duties, and it is intolerable: 'A moral system allows perplexity (or conflict of duties) *simpliciter* if and only if situations to which it applies are possible, in which somebody would find himself able to obey one of its precepts only if he violated another, even though he had up to then obeyed all of them.'[10] Hence Donagan believes all situations of moral conflict like we have discussed to be spurious and illusory.

But Donagan fails to see that moral conflicts that, to use his terminology, 'arise out of violations of duty,' are of two sorts: (1) those he described, where the violator, in virtue of what he has done, now finds himself unable to satisfy two moral precepts that apply to him, and (2) those where some other person or persons, in virtue of some violation that he (they) did not commit, now find that two precepts command two different actions which cannot both be performed. In this second sort of case, which I shall dub perplexity (or conflict) *secundum naturam*, the rationalist who sets himself to construct the system of moral precepts faces a kind of theoretical dilemma: if he coordinates the actions of persons under some assumption of general or ideal obedience to the precepts, then there will be cases of conflict of this second sort in a world like ours, where, by his own admission, perplexity *secundum quid* arises. But if he tries to implement design coordination by taking account of what people should do whenever they *would* be faced with perplexity *secundum naturam* – that is, if he tries to anticipate the difficulties in practice that a system of precepts based merely on an assumption of general (or ideal) observance would face, and uses this to modify the principles – he seems committed to attributing too great a capacity to us, to our knowledge of the course of events that constitutes the world. In short, to an epistemic ideality that can be satisfied only by creatures much more god-like than ourselves.[11]

Some loss of co-ordination seems endemic to the human

situation: it is something that is ineliminable save through an idealization that loses touch with that humanity and cannot be implemented in practice. Sidgwick's model of ideal rationality seems *so far removed*, so inapplicable to practice, that it distorts not just the rational nature of our practices, but the nature of our rational capacities. Hence I am inclined to believe that Sidgwick's conception of practical rationality and his corresponding conception of morality and moral judgement are profoundly misguided. Moral judgement and knowledge are represented in an asocial (and hence, ahistorical) manner. Moral judgement is taken to be the expression of a rule, a function, that is essentially a computing procedure. Consider, for a moment, a person of experience and good character: he characteristically reasons correctly about moral issues. Sidgwick cannot explain this fact. Why? Because he has no account of the connection between practical reasoning and character. He thinks of practical reasoning as mental computations to which are happily attached, by the providence of nature, moral personalities; their motivational structures are understood independently and thought to evolve independently.

According to this conception that Sidgwick advances, a moral theorist's task is to discover the rule (or set of rules) that characterizes the computing procedure; that rule (or set of rules) must, by its very nature, be capable of representation by an asocial entity, such as, for example, a computer. Here is a siren whose powers magnetize and beguile many: the idea that the heart of morality is to provide the procedure that connects these numerous acts to the various moral predicates that apply to them. The moral theorist's task is merely to provide the link, the standard, in virtue of which the subjects of moral judgement are associated with the correct predicates.

There is a certain anachronism in understanding Sidgwick's thought in the way it has been cast thus far. It is that notions such as computing procedures, algorithms, and functions are ways we can understand Sidgwick in terms not available to him. Such notions function as surrogates for the notion of the rule of law, and the corresponding juridical representations and analogies. The moral theorist is like the legislator who writes the laws. (It was no accident that Kant's moral thought was dominated by this sort of language.) His task, like that of the persons in the state-house, is to delineate standards that persons are to consult to determine how they should act. Of course, any of us can, so to speak, become legislators, if only hypothetically or in our imaginations: the conclusion of the social contract tradition – Hobbes, Locke, Kant – written large. Sound moral judgements are merely the conclusions at which competent moral judges would arrive. The key to moral philosophy, indeed the essence of the moral universe, is the moral codification that the best moral legislators would engrave in stone.[12] And the easiest way to uncover the key is to see how anyone becomes such a moral legislator.

This conception of moral rules that transcend us, no matter who we are or when or where we live, is something that must be scrutinized intensely; that will be done in due time. For now, however, I must content myself with saying that part of its attraction for many seems to lie just in its transcendent features. That, for instance, moral rules represent a timeless rational system open to any rational inquirer who will but assume an impersonal point of view: what Sidgwick called 'the point of view of the Universe.' To me, this is no attraction at all. Rather, it is a deep absurdity. It requires the unattainable: that human nature be permanent and un-changing; that the role of judgement – at least, human judgement – be eliminable from moral thought; that moral inquiry and thought begins only after the facts of the case have been certified; that the character of persons is irrele-vant to moral truth. Practical thought, practical judgement is identified with information manipulation. It is as if a 20th century computer programmer, who was most adept at get-ting his machine to process strings of numbers, now turned his attention to the task of processing the non-numerical information represented in strings of characters. The prob-lem is simply that this misidentifies the nature of practical thought, which is not confined to information manipulation, but must include the identification of facts relevant to moral assessments, developing conceptions of oneself and itself, and articulating both, and making these conceptions a reality. If there was one thing about which Kant was deeply right, it is that the will is practical reason; and hence (he should have said, rather than denying) there is a fundamental unity between thought, feeling, and perception. It is to these matters that we should now turn. Although slowly. Let's begin by seeing what someone deeply opposed to Sidgwick's embrace of Direct View might have to say.

III

Moral Virtues and the Direct View

———◆———

And here there occurs the fourth reflection which I purposed to make, in suggesting the reason why modern philosophers have often followed a course in their moral inquiries so different from that of the ancients. In later times, philosophy of all kinds, especially ethics, have been more closely united with theology than ever they were observed to be among the heathens; and as this latter science admits of no terms of composition, but bends every branch of knowledge to its own purpose, without much regard to the phenomena of nature, or to the unbiased sentiments of the mind, hence reasoning, and even language have been warped from their natural course, and distinctions have been endeavored to be established where the difference of objects was, in a manner, imperceptible. Philosophers, or rather divines under that disguise, treating all morals as on a like footing with civil laws guarded by the sanctions of reward and punishment . . .

Inquiry Concerning the Principles of Morals, 138

————————————

Aristotle, in denying that moral standards are representable as functions, or rules of the sort envisaged by Sidgwick, furnishes an illuminating account of one rendition of the Indirect View. To it we should now turn. After a brief detour, that is.

To understand Aristotle's advocacy of the Indirect View, it will be necessary, first, to do what philosophers today often think of themselves as doing best: making some distinctions. With these in hand we shall be better able to appre-

27

ciate the Aristotelian perspective and, more importantly, less likely to misinterpret it through our modern predilections.

It is a familiar feature of modern moral philosophy that an obvious focus is taken for granted: developing a systematic understanding of the principles of morality, where the 'principles of morality' is taken to refer to standards or norms that delineate conduct morally prohibited or obligatory, wrong or right. The historical tradition whose foremost advocates included Socrates, Plato, and Aristotle did not share this focus. They took it as obvious that a systematic understanding of moral virtues and vices was the epicenter of moral theory. Modern theorists have tended to view this older tradition as somewhat misguided, as foreign to us both culturally and philosophically. After all, it is said, these writers were not concerned with a person's obligations, or a person's duties, or what a person owes to society or other people, but with the cultivation of traits and character. For them morality was not a matter of rules or principles.

The debate between these two different approaches to moral philosophy has recently been renewed. Some have tried to reconcile the two seemingly disparate approaches; others have tried to provide arguments showing why neglect of this older tradition impoverishes modern moral philosophy.[1] In this chapter a contribution to this discussion is necessary in order to prepare a proper understanding of the challenge that Aristotle's thought presents to the Direct View, especially the modern versions of it which are most familiar. Specifically, I shall argue that accepted modern accounts of the role of virtues in moral theory – accounts that, if accurate, would prevent virtues from being a determinant of right action – are defective. Retiring these common misapprehensions about the relationships between virtues and acts will provide a theoretical groundwork for understanding why a virtue theorist such as Aristotle is not merely concerned with the good – as marked by a theory of the virtues – but with a theory of the right and the good, as marked by a theory of the virtues.

One of the recognized blemishes of modern moral philosophy, one that has recently been addressed, has been the tendency of moral philosophers to classify voluntary actions (or kinds of actions) under three headings: (1) acts that are duties, or obligatory, or required, or that we ought to perform, these terms and expressions being treated as synonymous; (2) actions that are forbidden, that we have a duty or an obligation not to do, from which we are required to refrain; and, (3) actions that are permissible, in the sense that they are neither obligatory nor forbidden.[2] Two sound lines of criticism have been advanced against this impoverished list of moral categories.[3] Let's review each.

Call these categories (respectively) the Morally Obligatory, the Morally Prohibited, and the Morally Indifferent. Are they adequate for capturing moral reality? No. Supererogatory acts exist. A soldier uses his body to shield his comrades from a hail of bullets, a neighbor rushes into the burning house to save his friend's child. These are acts of supererogation: often characterized as 'above and beyond the call of duty.' Such acts cannot be accommodated in an adequate manner by the categorical trinity. They certainly do not belong to the category of the Morally Obligatory. Nor to the Morally Prohibited. But it is misleading *in extremis* to place such acts in the category of the Morally Indifferent. Surely some morally favorable characterization should apply; these acts are not morally indifferent in the manner that, say, chewing bubble gum on the way to the store is.

Second, the trinity, though traditional in some circles, is baneful and obscurantist. Why? It encourages the practice of using the concept of moral obligation to cover every action for which we have moral reasons to perform (or forebear from performing). It is not unlike the presently popular idiom of the American populace for addressing moral questions: 'Does he have a right to it?' As if all moral questions concerned rights. Or obligations.

Why is this practice objectionable? What does it obscure? Recall that the Morally Obligatory is construed as a general classification that applies to actions (or kinds of actions) that are duties, or obligatory, or required, or that we ought to perform. And this is a mistake; these terms are not synonymous.[4] If they were, then a statement like 'I ought not to

29

fulfill my promise even though I am under a moral obligation to do so' should be bafflegab because it is self-contra-
dictory. But such statements are coherent. And, at times,
true. There are times when promises are to be broken and
there are moral grounds for doing so. They are not the rule,
of course, but no matter.

It would be a mistake to think that this criticism of the
Obligatory is merely a claim about meaning. The issue is
not verbal, only a matter of terminology. Other issues un-
derlie and are connected to this apparently semantic one.
For instance, a number of authors who make the mistake of
treating these various terms and expressions as synonymous
also deny the reality of moral conflicts. Ross, for one, defined 'right' as 'suitable, in a unique and indefinable way
which we may express by the phrase "morally suitable,"
to the situation in which the agent finds himself.'[5] And
since he then treated 'right' and 'duty' as synonymous, his
account of apparent moral conflict in terms of prima facie
duties degenerates into a denial of moral conflicts: all such
conflicts involve things that are not actually duties, but only
tend to be duties or, that is to say, are prima facie duties.[6]
Kant's position is similar.[7] Both hold there to be some
unique act that we can describe as the person's duty, or
obligation, or what is morally required of him, what he
ought to do. So there is a natural, even if not an essential,
connection between the semantic issue and systematic questions concerning the nature of moral reality.

It is not, however, the inadequacies of accounts that deny
the reality of moral conflict which shall now be the focus of
attention. We shall concentrate, at least for the moment, on
a different underlying issue. Namely, that treating these
various expressions as synonymous tends to conceal the fact
that morality has different dimensions or, so to speak, territories; these different expressions are associated, at least
partially, with these different territories, and hence the
treatment of them as synonyms tends to conceal their connections with their moorings.

Mill was one moralist who explicitly recognized, at times,
different dimensions or sources of morality that represent
how the cares, concerns, and interests of people secure a

place in our reasoning, thought, feelings; and that each dimension requires attention and a different sort of treatment by the moral theorist. In Chapter V of *Utilitarianism* he distinguished between justice and other 'obligations' of morality, saying that 'a right in some person, correlative to the moral obligation, constitutes the specific difference between justice and generosity or beneficence. Justice implies something which it is not only right to do, but which some individual can claim as his moral right. No one has a moral right to our generosity or beneficence because we are not morally bound to practice those virtues toward any given individual.'[8] Mill's distinction is between different sorts of virtues: that of justice – which concerns what people *owe* each other in the way of goods, service, and conduct – and virtues, like that of generosity and friendship, which concern goods that are not *owed* or *due* to one. To ignore this distinction, either by refusing to recognize virtues other than justice as morally significant or by claiming that justice is the whole of morality, is something one must do if they stick with the categorical trinity. More precisely, it is the sort of move to which one is coerced.

And it certainly has been the tendency of many post-Kantian philosophers to assimilate all virtues to what we can call the Requirements of Morality: acts that fall either under the Morally Obligatory or under the Morally Prohibited. After all, it is thought an obvious truism that the moral theorist's main task is to catalogue our moral duties and obligations. So, when confronted with the importance of acts of virtue that are not obligations or duties, such theorists refuse to recognize that the world fails to conform to their theoretical conceptions. Nonetheless, as a tacit recognition of this intransigence, they become willing to countenance 'special' duties or 'imperfect' duties. Thus they make the distinction, slyly and half-heartedly, between meritorious acts that are nonobligatory and those that are, by inflating the Requirements of Morality to include the former. In doing this they are following Kant, though perhaps unknowingly. For Kant was mesmerized by the model of law, of legal-like strict duties. When it was discovered that there is more to morality, the model was 'stretched,' the net result being the unwieldy philosophical fictions of 'perfect' and 'imperfect' duties, used to explain some mysterious distinction between kinds of duties or obligations.[9]

The Kantian distinction between perfect and imperfect duties was a modification of a distinction, referred to either as perfect and imperfect rights, or perfect and imperfect obligations, inherited from Grotius and Pufendorf. In the latter's work we find several different features associated with the distinction:

> It should be observed, in conclusion, that some things are due us by a perfect, and others by an imperfect right. When what is due us on the former score is not voluntarily given, it is the right of those in enjoyment of natural liberty to resort to violence and war in forcing another to furnish it, or, if we live within the same state, an action against him at law is allowed; but what is due on the latter score cannot be claimed by war or extorted by a threat of the law ... the reason why some things are due us perfectly and others imperfectly, is because among those who live in a state of mutual natural law there is a diversity in the rules of this law, some of which conduce to the mere existence of society, others to an improved existence. And since it is less necessary that the latter be observed towards another than the former, it is, therefore, reasonable that the former can be exacted more rigorously than the latter.[10]

This idea that virtues like gratitude, kindness, generosity, charity, and friendship are the 'extras' which make social life rich, not the ingredients that make social life possible, that they are secondary, not basic, that they are merely the ornamentation on the pillars of the social edifice, goes, I think, to the heart of the matter. For what is at issue is not how these virtues are named, but an assessment of their moral importance, of the scope they have in our moral life. Hume's genius, as we shall see, was to insist that there is no use for this distinction drawn in this manner: it is an objectionable part of the social contract tradition, a part that is contrary to historical and sociological realism. Hume saw clearly that the distinction has to do with segregating the moral dimensions of the activities of commerce and business: not the very existence of social life.

If the notion of duty or obligation is not expanded in the Kantian manner we are left with a minimalist morality. One that is incomplete. And, exactly why it is incomplete is the crux of a most weighty issue. What is the *nature of the moral value* exhibited in interesting moral cases (involving friendship, personal relations, virtues) not handled by a minimalist morality?

Let's consider such a case.[11] Your friend is in the hospital and, though you have no duty (in the colloquial sense of the term) to visit her, there are moral grounds for visiting her nonetheless. After all she is your *friend*.

If we return, momentarily, to the categorical trinity with which we began, we see that the act would fall under the category of the Morally Permissible: it would be something which you have no obligation to do or refrain from doing. It would be a matter of mere personal choice: what you are free to pursue, if you wish, since such conduct is neither prescribed nor proscribed by any principle of right. It is *merely permissible*.

But surely such a rendition is wrong. There is a fundamental moral difference between acts like, for example, chewing gum – acts lacking any morally significant value – and acts like comforting your friend because she's your friend. Hence the necessity of 'adding' something to this theory to account for the phenomena.

What more is to be allowed? One way to supplement the minimalist construction is to recognize that an account of morally desirable conduct, which is not itself morally required, must be added. That is the nature of the case at issue, is it not?

Perhaps. The exact nature of the moral value of the friend's visit is not, I think, accommodated under all versions of the proposed amendment. The minimalist morality would not be completed by saying that in such cases we can recognize that it would be morally permissible and desirable to perform this act, *and that's all*. Such an addition would be too weak: it would fail to provide an adequate understanding of the nature of the moral value of friendship. The philosophical and moral point about this and similar cases is that the person ought to visit his friend and it would be wrong to fail to do so.[12] It's not that it would (merely) be a morally good thing to do this. If the principles of right are to be exhaustive they, too, must bear on this and similar cases. Any ethic can express our common sense of the moral importance of acts of friendship and the relationships to which such acts are tied only if it acknowledges their value in relation to *both the right and human good*: they are indispensable for a human life that partakes of the good, that is good; and they are constitutive of the right in virtue of the role they play in the good.

This last claim is to be underscored. It is this double fact about these relationships and their accompanying activities – their double value – that, I think, is so often missed by modern moral philosophers.[13] How is this so?

Most 20th century moral theorists have crafted moral theories that are either teleological or deontological; and they tend to regard all theories as falling within one of these classifications. Certainly, however, this latter tendency is mistaken. A teleological theory is one in which the good is characterized independently from the right, and the right is characterized in terms of the good.[14] (In its simplest form one can think of such a theory as selecting some one value as the basis for all judgements of the good, and then proceeding to define the right as the maximization of the good already specified.) A teleological theory must provide an account of judgements of goodness that in no way refer to rightness. By contrast, in deontological theories the right is held to be logically prior to the good: the right constrains or restricts conceptions of the good, and is, in exactly that sense, the primary moral value. But notice, now, that this typology is not exhaustive. There remains a third type of theory: namely, one like that held by Aristotle, where human excellence (virtues) are held to provide some principles of right, but the right is not characterizable independently from the good, *nor vice versa*. The right and the good are held to be *interdependent*. Human excellences such as friendship and courage acquire their moral standing as constituents of human good, of a human life that flourishes, of practices and conventions that improve, enlighten, and ennoble our lives. But just as conceptions of justice, as principles of right, create limits for reasonable conceptions of human good, the full specification of the principles of right needs access to and is limited by a morally controversial conception of human good: the specification of our specific nature that grounds the conception of human good, which in turn funds the rightness of acts of friendship and other excellences. Such a view, which we shall develop in some detail through our examination, first of Aristotle, and subsequently of Hume, does challenge any deontological or teleological theory in a fundamental way: for it asserts that each gives the wrong account of the principles of right when it comes to understanding the moral value of friendship and other human excellences.

It might be objected that we have misunderstood the reason why many have taken virtues like generosity and friendship and referred to them, or the acts associated with them, as obligations. After all, there is a perfectly good sense of the word 'obligatory' which just means 'morally impermissible not to …'; this is its canonical use, for instance, in deontic logic. Hence if morality counsels us that failure to perform some act, as for example, an act of generosity, would be wrong, then it just follows that this act is obligatory.

Of course. *If* 'obligatory' has such a meaning,[15] then acts of virtue are often obligatory *in that sense*.[16] It in no way follows, though, that what is obligatory (in this sense) is an obligation or a duty, is to be classified as Morally Obligatory or Morally Prohibited. To think otherwise is to adopt a particular theory of the virtues on the basis of an equivocation.

There is a different – and many would argue, more compelling – reason why virtues like generosity and friendship have been given short shrift. It is the idea that the virtue of justice is the core of morality and these other virtues are really in no way comparable; they create no obligations or duties, and *cannot*; they have an altogether different status and role in morality.

How is this idea fleshed out? Often, as follows. Virtues,

it is said, are merely dispositions; they are merely desires or feelings. Consider, for example, some virtue. Take courage. What is it? Well, if you think long and hard, you will finally arrive at an answer that defines it as some sort of tendency. For instance, a tendency not to give in to one's fears in certain situations. But that shows that what's meant by virtues is nothing but some sorts of psychological inclinations of actors: something like good or bad motives. And *such things* do not inform us in any way what it is that, morally speaking, we ought to do; moreover, they cannot. In fact, whether *such things* are appraised positively or negatively from the moral point of view presupposes a prior understanding of the moral character of the acts with which they are associated. So not only is it true that psychological qualities, like virtues, provide no principles of morality, it is also true that what sorts of things in that category are found to be virtues – instead of vices – will be determined by the principles of morality. It follows that virtues can only play a secondary role in morality: say, that of supplementing our principles of moral obligation by insuring that we willingly do what the principles dictate. Virtues are merely the dispositions that provide the motivation to act on the principles of morality.

Such is the position of Frankena, who once suggested that 'for every principle there will be a morally good trait often going by the same name, consisting of a disposition or tendency to act according to it, and for every morally good trait there will be a principle defining the kind of action which is to express it. To parody a famous dictum of Kant's, I am inclined to think that principles without traits are impotent and traits without principles are *blind*.'[17] Indeed Frankena makes it somewhat clearer exactly why it is thought that virtues cannot play the important role assigned to principles of moral obligation. Principles (of duty) are basic because they define the morally relevant kinds of actions, and virtues are not to be taken seriously because they cannot play a primary role in action guidance. If they could, what Frankena calls an 'ethics of virtue' could provide a real alternative to what he calls an 'ethics of duty.' But Frankena rejects any full-blooded 'ethics of virtue,' defending and espousing, instead, an 'ethics of duty' that allows a diminished conception of an ethics of virtue – one which strips away the notion of virtues having any action guiding role:

> an ethics of duty or principles also has an important place for the virtues and must put a premium on their cultivation as a part of moral education and development. The place it has for virtue and/or the virtues, is however, different from that accorded them by an ethics of virtue. Talking in terms of the theory defended (earlier), which was an ethics of duty, we may say that, if we ask for *guidance* about what to do or not do, then the answer is contained, at least primarily, in ... the principles of beneficence and equal treatment. Given these two deontic principles, plus the necessary clarity of thought and factual knowledge, we can know what we morally ought to do or not do, except perhaps in cases of conflict between them. We also know that we ought to cultivate two virtues, a disposition to be beneficial (i.e., benevolence) and a disposition to treat people equally (justice as a trait). But the point of acquiring these virtues is not further guidance or instruction; the function of the virtues in an ethic of duty is not to tell of what to do but to ensure that we willingly do (our duty) ...[18]

Two points require attention. First, there is Frankena's contention that virtues cannot provide guidance about what it is that we should do. Second, there is an argument for this claim. Let's examine each.

The claim that virtues cannot provide action guidance, that they cannot instruct us about what to do, seems falsified by our ordinary moral experience. In what are commonly called decision contexts – situations wherein persons find themselves confronted with a choice between performing various alternative actions – it is a commonplace that we often make judgements like 'This would be the generous thing to do and it's what I ought to do,' or 'I shouldn't do that; it would be cowardly.' If I am faced with a choice I can quite naturally ask, 'Wouldn't doing this be greedy (dishonest, indecent, inconsiderate, uncivil)?,' 'What is the generous (honest, decent, considerate, civil) thing to do?'

And, often enough, we answer such questions. Correctly. So our moral experience suggests that virtues provide action guidance, at least in the same sense in which, say, the principle of beneficence or the principle of equal treatment provides action guidance. Our moral experience indicates that virtues are, in this respect, no better or worse off than moral obligations and duties and the principles that characterize them.

We can and do identify acts as morally obligatory. Hence we believe that a moral theory should be able to tell us how to identify these acts, and thereby guide our selections of acts in decision contexts. (How a moral theory accomplishes this identification is, of course, a matter of some contention.) But the case with the virtues is identical. We can and do identify acts as instances of particular virtues. Hence a moral theory should be able to tell us how to identify these acts, and thereby guide our selection of acts in decision contexts. Question: why has this second matter – how one goes about identifying acts of virtue – received but scant philosophical attention in the 20th century, even though it is on a par with the equivalent task concerning moral obligations? Does our moral experience deceive us? Or what?

The argument for the claim that virtues cannot guide or instruct us about what to do contains the answer, perhaps. But we should not review the argument, as it were, narrowly. We should look at it as being connected to a metaphysical perspective that generates it. We should be aware that we are not simply confronting an argument, but a legion of ideas.

Recall that the Direct View makes actions (or kinds of actions) the business of moral theory. Behind this claim lies a sharp distinction between acts and motives:[19] what Lawrence Blum has labeled the schema of act and motive,[20] namely, that what makes an act right must be independent of the motive(s) that led to the performance of that act. A central claim of the schema is that the *same* act could be performed from different motives (some good, some not) and still be right: motives are held irrelevant to the assessment of an act's rightness. Appraisals of acts and motives are held to be logically independent. What's more, the identification of any particular act as the act it is cannot refer, implicitly or explicitly, to its motivation. Any such reference would violate the principle that the *same* act can be performed from different motives.

Such is a kernel of a metaphysical view of behaviorism: that only outward behavior is fully real; that acts are fully real and nothing 'inward' is; that questions about motives and feelings are secondary and must be addressed in terms of what is fully real if one is not to go astray. Inner experiences, aspects of the inner world of the psyche must be understood in terms of the outer. For instance, desires are analysed as tendencies or dispositions that are identified with certain behavior patterns; they are, in reality, nothing more than the behavior patterns. Such is the metaphysical view of the behaviorist.[21]

A key assumption, then, of the argument that purports to show that virtues cannot provide action guidance is its insistence that virtues be defined as dispositions or tendencies to act in certain ways. And it is an assumption that has not gone unchallenged.[22]

Nonetheless, suppose, for purposes of argument, we grant that virtues are dispositions or tendencies to perform virtuous acts. What, precisely, is the objection to virtues under such an assumption? Well, since a virtue could not be identified independently of the acts which are its manifestations, moral theory could not require both that we be of a certain character and that we perform certain kinds of acts. For to be of a certain character would just be to perform certain kinds of acts. Hence virtues could not be valuable in themselves; they could be valuable, as Frankena has it, only for the acts they are tendencies to produce. Thus the ontology brought forth by the metaphysics of behaviorism dictates what can be valuable in itself. (Another example of how bad moral philosophy is grounded in bad metaphysics and philosophy of mind.)

To continue. Still granting that virtues are merely dispositions, we might put the following dilemma to a theorist sympathetic to the virtues. Either the acts which are the manifestations of virtues have value independently of the way they are brought into existence or they do not. Suppose, first, that they do. Since virtues are not and cannot be valuable in themselves, we can only identify particular tendencies *as virtues* (or, as vices, or as neither) by reference to the right or the good. It follows that the identification of particular dispositions as virtues depends upon a prior determination of the right or the good. Hence particular virtues cannot themselves be determinants of the right or the good; thus it is fitting that they be given a secondary status. On the other hand, suppose that virtuous acts do not have value independently of the way they are brought into existence: the moral value of the motives of the agent must be the sole basis for attributing value to the acts of virtue. This is a position like that of Martineau, who held that the moral value of the motives of the agent is the fundamental determinant of right action.[23] Such a view is patently false. Acts can be morally right even if performed from an 'improper' motive.

Such is the dilemma, grounded as it is in bad psychology. Martineau's view is intriguing because it tries to invert the view it challenges, without rooting out the very assumptions that make that view so problematic. Rather than saying the moral appraisal of acts, independently of the motives that may have produced them, is primary, he boldly reversed the order. But his is a move that is doomed, since it is embedded in the same bad metaphysics and psychology that creates the dilemma. One should take notice of it and study it with care, nonetheless; for it is much like Kant's attempt to derive rightness from a certain type of motivational structure – that of a good will – and comparison of the two views is enlightening.

The dilemma is easily evaded by moral theorists who are not wedded to the misconceptions that ground it. The first step is merely the rejection of the analysis of virtues as dispositions. Everyone agrees that the analysis of particular virtues must include essential reference to beliefs and desires: the ascription of a particular virtue (e.g., courage) to a person relies, essentially, on the understanding that he possesses certain beliefs and desires. (More on this shortly.) But if we consider the concepts of belief and desire, they are best understood as theoretical concepts that get their sense from the role they play in a network of generalizations used in the explanation of human action.[24] Neither desires nor beliefs are uniquely identifiable with a disposition to perform some item or pattern of publicly observable behavior. And, as with desires and beliefs, so with character traits that are virtues: they cannot be identified with dispositions either. Hence we have no reason not to maintain that (i) virtues can be both valuable in themselves and for the acts they produce, and (ii) that moral theory can require both that we be of a certain character and perform certain kinds of acts. Moral theory can hold that human good consists both in virtuous action and in being a person of a certain character.

What is it to be a person of a certain character? How is character related to virtues and vices? How are virtues and vices related to psychological states like beliefs and desires? It is to questions such as these, and to Aristotle's treatment of the virtues that we should now turn.

IV

Aristotle: The Indirect View

———————◆———————

We may remark, then, that every virtue or excellence both
brings into good condition the thing of which it is the excellence
and makes the work of that thing be done well ... Therefore ...
the virtue of man also will be the state of character that makes a
man good and which makes him do his own work well.

Nicomachean Ethics, 1106a16–24

The manner in which Aristotle treats moral virtues or
human excellences[1] is most instructive. He avoids a faulty
dispositional analysis by insisting that these traits must be
understood on analogy with the character of individuals.
Predicates such as 'courageous,' 'generous,' 'honest,' and
'unselfish,' apply, in the first instance, to persons. Not
actions. The behavioristic analyses favored so often by
modern writers impale themselves on this very point. These
terms are used primarily for properties of *persons*, and only
secondarily – only through reference to their primary usage
– to properties of actions. As Aristotle put the case: 'Actions
then are called just and temperate when they are such as
the just or temperate man would do; but it is not the man
who does these that is just and temperate, but the man who
does them as the just and temperate men do them.'[2]
  The very notion of a courageous act – taking courage to
be our paradigm for moral virtues, for the moment – is
secondary to and dependent upon the notion of a courageous person. The former acquires its sense from the latter.
How so? An act gets rightly called courageous when and
only when it is such that the courageous person would per-

42

form it in those circumstances. The courageous man is thought of as an ideal type, who is the exemplar of courage; it is by reference to that type that we select which acts are typical of courage. Once we have, so to speak, got our hands on such an exemplar, we can, by reference to what he would do, decide whether what we and others do is in fact courageous. That task, of appraising the courageousness of acts, relies essentially on our understanding of the trait of courage, a characteristic of a type of person. It is by understanding how the choices, desires, values, emotions, actions, and will of such a person cohere into a whole – a unity that we refer to as a type of character – that we understand the virtue of courage. And how a human excellence makes *both* an agent and his action good.

The unity of character is extremely labyrinthine. It couples systematically a person's values, choices, desires, strength or weakness of will, emotions, feelings, perceptions, interests, expectations, and sensibilities. If a person is generous, there are certain things he must care about, take an interest in, want to achieve. If a person is honest he must recognize certain sorts of considerations as reasons for acting and must act on certain sorts of considerations. If a person is courageous, he will feel certain sorts of emotions under certain conditions: guilt in some, distress in others, relief in yet others. A compassionate person is not only disturbed by other people's distress, but is more sensitive to why and when others may be distressed.[3] A compassionate person is not only motivated to relieve such distress, but is also discomforted by the (unrelieved) distress because he cares about the comfort and well-being of others; in this way compassion is expressed not only in action because of what is thought and felt, but expressed in feeling and thought. Clearly, then, these types of character are psychological leviathans that involve intricate, interwoven connections between desires, emotions, feelings, reasoning, perception, capacities, sensitivities, and action.

The elaborate and systematic unity of types of character underscores both the bankruptcy of modern views – that, for example, analyze such traits of character wholly as dispositions or desires – and the brilliance of writers like Plato and Aristotle, who maintained that character traits are best understood as the connected patterns of thought, feeling, and action that types of persons exemplify. Generosity does not merely involve acting and thinking and feeling in a certain way; the action is undertaken because of what is thought and felt; what is felt is due to what is thought and perceived; what is thought and perceived would be different were it not for what is the focus of concern and feeling. The different aspects of the psychological edifice are like the 'parts' of a maelstrom: there is systematic interconnectedness. There is no basic part, no part which is prior to the rest. It is a mistake to ask, 'But isn't the character type really a construct of reason (or feeling)?'

Which is not to say that nothing can be said about the elements. Aristotle held that what makes an act correctly called generous is that it is what the generous person would do in those particular circumstances. Call such acts *typical* of a virtue:[4] they are the sort of thing a courageous or honest person would do in such circumstances, however they might be motivated in a particular case. Such an act, an act that is *typical* of some virtue, need not *exhibit* that virtue. That is to say, acts typical of virtues need not exhibit the virtues of which they are typical; one need not be a generous person, for example, to perform on some occasion an act that is truly generous. A coward may, on occasion, muster his reserves, overcome his fear, and do the courageous thing; but this does not make him a courageous man. The latter acts this way as a matter of course or second nature. Only persons who perform acts of virtue as the exemplar of that virtue does are themselves said to be persons of that type.

In what does the difference between exhibiting a virtue and merely performing an act typical of that virtue consist? Aristotle cites three conditions an act must satisfy if it is to exhibit the agent's excellence or virtue: '... if acts which are in accordance with human excellences have themselves a certain character, it does not follow that they are done justly or temperately. The agent must also be in a certain condition when he does them; in the first place he must have knowledge, secondly, he must choose the acts, and choose them for their own sakes, and thirdly, his action must proceed from a firm and unchangeable character.'[5]

The three conditions cited by Aristotle are provisions for the possession of a moral virtue; they are conditions that an agent must satisfy if his act is to exhibit his excellence. Let's examine them.

Take the third condition. The claim that the character must be unalterable is amiss; but what is meant by saying the action must proceed from a firm character? This notion of firmness is best understood as a requirement needed because the first two conditions are inadequate by themselves. And why is that? Why cannot they stand by themselves? The issue, as Aristotle sees it, is that the motive condition – 'the acts must be chosen for their own sakes' – specifies the type of psychological structure a person of a certain character must have, but does not guarantee that the action actually is a result and expression of that type. For example, a person might be miserly, yet on a given occasion overcome that state and perform an act typical of generosity for the very sort of reasons that a generous person would. Clearly, when this happens, the person is not transformed into a generous person. He does not yet regularly and firmly possess the outlook, values, and motivational structure of a generous person. Even though his motive was in this case just like that of the generous person's, at least in the sense that there was no ulterior motive and the act was chosen for its own sake.[6]

Let's try to be more precise about why we should not say that this miser's conduct is an expression of the motivational structure of a person who is generous, who is the type of person of which the act is typical.

Consider, first, those traits of character that we call virtues or excellences. If an act is to exhibit the agent's excellence, the agent must be principled: if he is, for example, courageous, he must be firmly committed to the dictates of courage; he must have a firm resolve to follow them; he must have the strength of will to act accordingly even when he has some inclination not to do so.[7] In short, he must *identify* himself as courageous, and this identification cannot be fraudulent. He must, therefore, see courage as furnishing a benchmark for evaluating his actions, as well as others', and must take that gauge to heart in the formation of his choices, attitudes, sentiments, and conduct.[8]

To fathom just what this makes the person like, consider what he is not like. If he possesses an excellence of character, he is not like someone who lacks that excellence. What is it that the second person lacks? Take a particular example. Say, dishonesty. Assume for the moment that dishonesty is characterized by the fact that the dishonest person is not committed to the principle that he ought to tell the truth or to the principle that he ought not to deceive people. How can this lack of commitment show?

In at least two ways: through a lack of resolve or the failure to act accordingly even when resolve is not lacking.

Consider each. First, consider a creature we shall call the Pliable Dodger. The Pliable Dodger believes that he ought to tell the truth, that he ought not to engage in deceit. He has a commitment – of sorts – to the principles of honesty; but he is weak willed. Often enough, he does things that he knows he ought not to do. He is dishonest. He performs dishonest acts. Contrary desires and inclinations often prevail. (He feels blameworthy later, no doubt, but the guilt does not suffice to make him more able to withstand seduction.)

Consider, second, a creature that we shall call the Machiavellian Dodger. He simply lacks any allegiance to the principles of honesty. The fact that some course of action requires lying or deceit is a consideration which, by itself, has no weight for the Machiavellian Dodger. If he sees some reason for lying, he will, other things being equal, lie. He will not be averse to lying because it is lying; that fact carries no weight with him.

Both of these Dodgers perform dishonest acts. Dishonest acts that exhibit their character: their dishonesty. But they do not exhibit that dishonesty in the same way, for they are deficient in honesty in different ways. The Pliable Dodger has the right desires and would choose rightly were he not weak willed. He is well meaning, but nonetheless dishonest – though not dishonest in the strict sense. His vice is a vice in a qualified sense; his deficiency in honesty is explainable by his weakness of will[9] and does not epitomize the vice of dishonesty.[10] Even the Machiavellian Dodger is not the 'purest embodiment' of dishonesty: it is the Libertine Dodger who satisfies this description. And what is he like? Well, he is like the Machiavellian Dodger in that he, too, lacks a commitment to the principles of honesty. But unlike his cousin, he opposes those principles; his loyalties are, as it were, those of the Pliable Dodger but inverted. (He 'knows' that this stuff about honesty is rubbish – a smoke-screen put up by the hypocritical and powerful to better themselves.) Hence it will be true both of the Machiavellian Dodger and the Libertine Dodger that the fact that some course of action requires lying is a consideration that, by itself, carries no weight against performing that act. But for the Libertine Dodger, unlike the Machiavellian Dodger, such a consideration does carry some weight: the reverse of that which it carries for the honest person. The Libertine Dodger cares for that the act is dishonest, but his care is inverted. The Machiavellian doesn't care a bit.

The Dodger family reveal what it is like to possess an excellence of character that is the opposite of a character defect like dishonesty. To possess and exhibit the excellence of character one must not be deficient in any of the ways various Dodger family members are. To possess some excellence of character, then, requires that one have a firm character: an enormously elaborate set of psychological states that meld systematically. A chronicle of that character must expose the connections and relations between the person's will, choices, values, sentiments, perceptiveness, appraisals, sensibilities, and conduct. No small matter, that.

One upshot of Aristotle's account of moral virtues, and their relationship to acts representative of them, is an insight into where an account like Martineau's goes astray. Recall, Martineau inverts a major claim of the Direct view – that the moral evaluation of acts is primary – by contending that the moral value of the motives of the agent is the fundamental determinant of right action. But we can see most readily that some virtuous acts, namely, those typical of the virtue, have value independently of how they are brought into existence. An act that is typical of charity is an estimable and praiseworthy act even if it is not characteristically motivated. To be sure, if it were characteristically motivated, the act would reflect credit on the moral estimate of the *agent* – credit that would not be reflected if, for instance, the act were performed from an 'improper' or 'unworthy' motive. But, to impugn the person's motives successfully is not to destroy the moral value of his act, at least not if the act was typical of a virtue.

'But,' one might now object, 'aren't you having it both ways? Does the Aristotelian account allow that acts *typical* of a virtue exclude *all* reference to motivation? If so, doesn't it imply a sharp distinction between an act, as something external, and a motive, as something internal? The very sort of sharp distinction that has been denied?'

The matter is not as clear as one would like. But I am inclined to answer that acts typical of a virtue acquire their value independently of how they are brought into existence. And in this sense they do not at all refer to the *motivation of the agent* who performed them. Nonetheless, I do think that what acts they are includes *some reference to motivation*: just not the motivation of the agent who performed them. And, I do not think that this implies a sharp act/motive distinction. For, on the one hand, someone who insists that there is such a sharp distinction is committed to the idea that there is a fixed way to 'divide up' events into acts, which are 'external' events and motives, which are 'internal' events that give rise to acts; and that this division can be accomplished in the same way in any context. But the fact of the matter is that through our conventions we classify acts into types for many different purposes. *Sometimes*, we group them just in the way that the advocate of a sharp distinction asserts. *But not always*. Some classifications are based on the characteristic purpose of the acts, others on their characteristic motives, yet others on their characteristic effects. There is no one schema (to use Blum's terminology) for understanding the phenomena. And, on the other hand, there is a 'historical' reference to motivation in the classification of acts typical of a virtue.

Consider Mr Priori, who donates a large sum to a charity, who does so intentionally, whose intention is that these funds shall help alleviate the suffering of the homeless in

New York City. His motive need not be a concern for the homeless; he may be seeking, through this action, an enhancement of his own reputation, a chance to enter the Social Register. Now we evaluate him differently from Smith, who acts solely from concern for the homeless. We evaluate Priori more like someone who contributes money to charity both because it is a charity and he needs a tax write-off. For like a caring tax dodger, he has intentionally done something that is good to have done. He's certainly done something *better* than if he had thrown a party with the funds, just as the tax dodger has done something better than investing the money in some venture that has no social benefits, but an equivalent tax benefit. Nonetheless Priori merits no moral approval, even if his act merits it.

Take this example of charity. I'm inclined to say that in some more rudimentary social order from which we have evolved, acts typical of charity would require some reference to the motivation that brought them about. That is to say, the description of the act as one *of charity* could not be established independently of some reference to motivation, either of the agent who performed it (in the first instance) or (at a later stage) to the characteristic motivation from which such acts are performed. But, *now*, we find ourselves in a different social situation from our ancestors. We have familiar and complex social institutions, practices, and rituals that help us to understand when acts of charity are likely to occur, how they can be encouraged, and so on. And, we understand classifications of such acts as acts of charity by reference to their *characteristic motivations* (in the sense I develop in this chapter), and not by reference to the actual motivation of the agent who performs such an act. Hence we can now recognize individual acts to be *typical of charity* without reference to the motivation of the agent who performed the act. (Though not without reference to the agent's intention.) Hence the appearance of this classification, which, on its face, seems to confirm the sort of line pushed by an advocate of a sharp distinction between act and motive, is, in fact, quite at odds with the account given by such advocates. For reference to types of character is essential to the classification of some acts.

Unlike the Direct View, both Aristotle and Martineau make moral evaluations of agents basic. But the fate of Martineau's strategy is sealed at the start; for he embraces the characterization of the distinction between the moral evaluation of acts and the moral evaluation of agents that adherents of the Direct View advance, but then claims that the priorities must be reversed. The result is his conviction that it is the value of the motives or character of the person who is in a deliberative context that is to be taken as the fundamental determinant of what action is right. His theory is agent-based, whereas the Direct View will always provide action-based theories. But notice that Aristotle's theory is agent-based as well. For it takes virtues and moral character seriously, claiming that a determinant of right action is the choice that a character of a certain type would make. That is, after all, the manner in which it identifies acts typical of moral virtues. Hence it differs from Martineau's account in several matters of considerable substance. First, it takes *types* of character as basic, not the *actual* agents who are found in deliberative contexts. It is from what the type would do that an inference is made about what the actual person should do. Second, it does not claim that the character of agents (or types of agents) is the determinant of right action, but only that it is a determinant.

Aristotle's theory is an example of a theory by a proponent of the Indirect View. It maintains that principles of moral virtue take types of agents as basic: particular acts of virtue are to be identified on the basis of what these sorts of agents would do. And since these principles require not just the performance of certain kinds of acts, but that we *be persons of a certain type – that we be of a certain character –* these are different sorts of practical principles than those addressed by traditional theorists like Sidgwick: a difference that has at times been vaguely captured by contrasting the 'morality of being' and the 'morality of doing.'

It is a further specification and clarification of such differences that we should now turn.

V

Further Reflections on Acts and Agents

—————————— ◆ ——————————

The good will is not good because of what it effects or
accomplishes or because of its adequacy to achieve some
proposed end; it is good only because of its willing ... Even if it
should happen that, by a particularly unfortunate fate or by the
niggardly provision of a stepmotherly nature, this will should be
wholly lacking in power to accomplish its purpose, and if even
the greatest effort should not avail it to achieve anything of its
end ... it would sparkle like a jewel in its own right, as
something that had its fullest worth in itself.

Foundations of the Metaphysics of Morals, Ak. 394

—————————————————

The schema of act and motive, shared by Sidgwick and
Martineau, was widely accepted by any number of writers
in the 18th and 19th centuries. Indeed, it seems a natural
concomitant of a moral theory that has as its guidepost the
rule of law. In this chapter I wish to discuss several such
writers, namely, Richard Price, Thomas Reid, and John
Stuart Mill, to illustrate further details of the schema. And,
to highlight its connection with accompanying metaphysical
and epistemological theses. As always, securing a proper
grasp of the differences between such views and versions of
the Indirect View is the goal.

A good starting point for our inquiry is Richard Price's
Review of the Principal Questions in Morals; in Chapter
VIII, in discussing the distinction between absolute and
practical virtue, there is a meticulous presentation of the
received distinction between the virtue of the action and the
virtue of the agent.[1] Price begins by distinguishing abstract

51

virtue, which he declares to be 'a quality of the external action or event. It denotes what an action is, considered independently of the *sense* of the agent; or what, in *itself* and *absolutely*, it is right *such* an agent, in *such* circumstances, should do; and what, if he judged truly, he would judge he ought to do.'[R, 177] What Price refers to as practical virtue, by contrast, 'has a necessary relation to, and dependence upon, the opinion of the agent concerning his actions.' [R, 177] Price acknowledges this distinction to be not unlike that often made between the formal and material goodness of actions. That distinction – descending from Aristotle's fourfold division of causes as transformed, first, under Stoic, and later, under Scholastic thought – does seem to represent the same, or a comparable, distinction. An action considered formally is what the agent intended to do. An action considered materially is one considered without any reference to the agent's state of mind in performing the act. Thus it was commonly thought that an action that was not materially good could well be formally good: for example, that of a physician who honestly (but wrongly) believed that he should lie to you about the state of your health, or that of a sheriff who incarcerates a man against his will solely for his own good.

In the 19th and 20th centuries this distinction seems to have been renamed once again. Moralists now commonly distinguish between the 'objective rightness' and the 'subjective rightness' of actions, meaning by the former the quality that the action has independently of whether it is thought to possess it by the agent, and by the latter, the qualities an agent possesses when he performs an act he takes to be right. The distinction is imported to prevent both a type of moral solipsism and the harsh moral view that all moral errors are blameworthy. As Price so aptly remarked, 'This distinction indeed cannot be rejected, without asserting, that whatever we *think* things to be, that they *are*, that we can in *no sense*, ever do wrong, without incurring guilt and blame; that while we follow our judgements, we cannot *err* in our conduct.' [R, 178]

What is the relation between this distinction of abstract and practical virtue to the distinction between the virtue of the act and the virtue of the agent? Reid, in the section of *Essays on the Active Powers* that parallels Chapter VIII of Price's *Review*, seems to think this is one distinction, differently named:

> We ascribe moral goodness to actions considered abstractly without any relation to the agent. We likewise ascribe moral goodness to an agent on account of an action he has done; we call it a good action, though, in this case, the goodness is properly in the man, and is only a figure ascribed to the action. Now, it is to be considered whether *moral goodness*, when applied to an action considered abstractly, has the same meaning as when we apply it to a man on account of that action . . .[2]

In this verdict Price and Reid stand in concord.[3] And disarray. Both fail to distinguish between intention and motive; both fail to see that an intention is identified with an action (in prospect) except in one situation, namely, when the action has already occurred. An act is distinguished from intention only if the act has already been performed; and even then, it is distinguished only elliptically.[4] We form intentions by considering various courses of action open to us, by considering their nature and what will result from them. The act we intend is the act we choose. Which is to say the object of the intending – what we call the intention – is some prospective act. When we do distinguish the act from the intention, the act must have already occurred. And the distinction between act and intention in such cases is elliptical; what is being distinguished is not the intention and the act, *per se*, but instead what act was performed and what act was the intended one. We want to know whether the act that was performed was the act that was intended, whether the act chosen was the act performed. Hence we are not, in fact, distinguishing the intention and the (prospective) act.

People commonly think that the act cannot be identified with the intention, since they take the two to be causally related. How does this happen? Take an ordinary case. Dennis embarrasses Martha by reading a memo to the group, a memo she had written that reveals her awareness of facts, ones about which she just avowed ignorance. Did Dennis intend to mortify her? Did he intend to set the record straight? The pattern commonly broached as manifestly suitable for addressing questions of this sort is: here is his act; its character is clear; but his intention is not; it's hidden. What is its character? What moved him to perform this act? What did he believe, take himself to be doing, find desirable?

One who accepts this format as the appropriate one for understanding intentions has been seduced by the ellipsis. For the character of Dennis's act is not apparent at all if we make no background assumptions about his intention: what he chose to do, what he knew, what he foresaw. The questions raised about his intention do not invite us to seek a hidden cause of his action, but to address the background assumptions that we have made in identifying what his act was. The questions demand that we attend to these assumptions further, to ensure that we have correctly identified his intention. If, for instance, we discover that Dennis was unaware of Martha's deceit, we know that he did not intend to cause chagrin or, for that matter, to correct the record. In turn, our understanding of what Dennis did changes; we now understand what he was about differently.[5]

To return to Price and Reid. Both treat intention as a mental cause of action. In doing so, both reveal their Cartesian heritage, treating intention as if it were part of the mental – namely, a mental state – that causes an 'external' act in the world of the physical. The core of the Cartesian stance on intention is that action is the expression of something 'inner' that must be discovered before we can correctly interpret the behavior of the actor. It is like the view that speech is the expression of something 'inner' that must be discovered to interpret linguistic behavior correctly. Thus the dualism of virtue Price and Reid endorse is grounded in different dualism: the metaphysical dualism of Cartesianism and its dualistic psychology, the radical separation of the sphere of the mind and that of the body. Only thought – including here, under *pensée*, *all* of the soul's operations – is avowed to be entirely within one's powers:

There is nothing entirely within our power except our thoughts; at least if you take the word 'thought' as I do, for all the operations in the soul, in such a way that not only meditations and acts of the will, but even the functions of sight and hearing, and the resolving of one movement rather than another, in so far as they depend on the soul, are all thoughts.[6]

In trying to clarify further the sense in which virtue attaches to actions and the sense in which in attaches to agents, Price seems especially taken in, sounding like Descartes himself:

it may possibly be of some advantage towards elucidating this matter, to conceive that only as, in strict propriety, *done* by a moral agent, which he *intends* to do. What arises beyond or contrary to his intention, however it may eventually happen, or be derived by the connexion of natural causes, from his determination, should not be imputed to him. Our own determinations alone are, most properly, our actions. These alone we have absolute power over, and are responsible for ... there are two views or senses in which we commonly speak of actions. Sometimes we mean by them, the determinations or volitions themselves of a being of which the intention is an essential part: And sometimes we mean the real event, or external effect produced. [184–185]

The Cartesian theme – that only the sphere of thought (where thought, or *pensée*, is given the ludicrous interpretation of referring to any mental or psychological operation) is within our power – is carried to yet another of its absurdities by Price. Actions must be things under our control, things that we effect; hence the 'real' and 'primary' acts must be entirely mental. All 'external' behavior is, in a 'fundamental' sense, really nothing but behavior; it is certainly not *action* in the fullest sense of the word.[7] Such is the view that the essence of life is lived internally: a view, I suspect, that would never arise except in a community of persons who share that aspiration for beatitude, for a union with (a Christian) God (or some metaphysical entity with comparable properties), that one finds in a range of people from the early Gnostics to the Protestant Reformers. To take that thought seriously and to heart is to enter a different community from ours.

To be sure, Price and Reid were in flight from the medieval theory of natural law which, in its classical formulation by Aquinas, held the necessary and eternal truths of morality to be based in the will of God.[8] But that flight can be both overstated and misstated. We must distinguish between the role a conception of God (or some surrogate) plays in moral thought and the secular intentions of an author. A secular moralist can craft a theory in which the conception of God is unwanted and unconceived, and yet, nevertheless, needed to support the theoretical edifice. For instance, a rationalist moral theory that views moral principles as an expression of divine law will be able to maintain a system of principles that is unitary and complete, if only because it can rely on the claim that all events are governed by God's will and express his providence. If the secular theorist removes the conception of God, but lets his understudy, man, play a comparable role, then there is a distinction without a difference. And such, I think, is the heart of moral theorists who espouse a secular rationalism. Reason becomes the creative will of God. We, as creatures of reason, are not merely the center of the moral universe: we are its creators. The moral universe, and all its problems, are to be governed and solved through our rational wills. So union with God need not be union with a Christian God. It can be a secular one. It is the conception of the path to perfection to which one should attend: 'Be ye therefore perfect, even as your Father which is in heaven is perfect.'[9]

Take note then. When Price and Reid and other moralists-cum-Cartesian-psychologists address the issue of what judgements of moral rightness are *about*, their dualistic psychology serves as a necessary backdrop for their views. Are moral judgements *about* the *external* character of the agent's behavior, or its *inner* origins? It is assumed that we can effortlessly segregate the 'external' and the 'inner,' so that this question can be addressed readily, no matter how much we might labor in a quest for the correct answer.

The Cartesian separation of the psyche and the world of bodily movements is built into the language in which the question is put: we are only a step away from adding that the mind is the authoritative director (the Cartesian pilot) that governs the body (the ship) through its will. Or, that since it cannot govern the body directly – that being part of the phenomenal world subject to a different sort of causality – and it must do so in a special and unique way: perhaps by providing an empirical motive produced by something nonempirical, namely, pure practical reason.

The conclusion of this line of reasoning, when pursued ambitiously, is indicated by Price and is elaborated by Kant. There is a fundamental sense in which the virtue of the act and the virtue of the agent must be the same. Price does not actually draw the conclusion; but he is, oh, so close. As he *almost* says, if our intentions alone are, most properly, actions – as contrasted with the external effects – then the virtue of the *act in this sense* is identical to the virtue of the agent; actions end up being internal characteristics of agents. The Kantian development of this theme, which might be best called the Cartesian Indirect View (for the primacy which it attaches to *agency* is Cartesian), provides a theoretical alternative both to advocates of the Direct View like Bentham and Sidgwick, and advocates of the Indirect View like Aristotle. It will demand a more detailed treatment shortly; for now, suffice it to note its metaphysical grounds.

Thus far the discussion of Price and Reid has centered on the psychological theory upon which they rely in marking the distinction between the virtue of the act and the virtue of the agent, between practical and absolute virtue, in Price's favored terminology. We should now attend to their failure to distinguish motive from intention, which causes further difficulties. Both hold that in evaluating acts – external pieces of behavior – consideration of the goodness of intentions, or motives, or character traits is irrelevant: such considerations have to do with agent evaluations and are only figuratively imputed to the act. Their view relies, therefore, on the correctness of the assumption that all evaluations of the moral merit of acts can be *grounded independently* of the moral evaluation of the merit of any agent. And it is exactly this assumption that seems false. (Especially so, given the manner that the distinction between the virtue of the act and the virtue of the agent is drawn.) We have seen how Aristotle challenged it; we will see how both Hume and Kant, in their different ways, deny it. A general challenge to the assumption need not be mounted to see the present difficulties, though. For, if no distinction between motive and intention is made, the assumption will need be violated. Why? Because no act is morally praiseworthy unless it is done with good intention. However, consideration of whether an agent's intention is good is a type of agent evaluation. Therefore, the moral evaluation of some acts to determine whether they are praiseworthy, whether they have moral merit relies on an agent evaluation.

Such a conclusion can be avoided, of course, if one draws a distinction between motive and intention. You merely allow the obvious that: that a meritorious act always requires good intention. But, you insist that intention is merely used to identify the action correctly; the evaluations of act and agent are distinct and separate; the former concerns absolute virtue, as Price said, but the latter concerns an evaluation of the agent that is grounded in an evaluation of the motive that led him to perform the act in question. Such is the tack of Mill and Bentham.

'It is the business of ethics to tell us what our duties are, or by what test we may know them,' wrote Mill in Chapter II of *Utilitarianism*.[10] But, he continued, utilitarians, unlike others, have been steadfast and vociferous in 'affirming that the motive has nothing to do with the morality of the action, though much with the worth of the agent. He who saves a fellow creature from drowning does what is morally right, whether his motive be duty or the hope of being paid for his trouble; he who betrays the friend that trusts him is guilty of a crime, even if his object be to serve another friend to whom he is under a greater obligation.' In a footnote to the second edition (1864), a footnote that was dropped from all later editions, Mill further clarified his position by addressing an objection raised by the Rev. J. Llewellyn Davies. Davies challenged Mill's claim that acts like that of saving a drowning person are morally right, no matter from what motive they are performed; a counter-instance is easily found, Davies asserted, in the act of a tyrant who saves his enemy from drowning in order that he may torture him. Mill's response is that Davies failed to distinguish motive from intention: 'The morality of the action depends entirely upon the intention – that is, upon what the agent *wills to do*. But the motive, that is the feeling which makes him will so to do, if it makes no difference in the act, makes none in the morality: though it makes a great difference in our moral estimation of the agent ...' Hence Mill holds that the tyrant's act of saving his enemy is not a true counterinstance to his claim, since it is a different act (or kind of act) from the one he described.[11]

Mill's answer, to be sure, is thoroughly uninformative, or worse. To be consistent Mill must either claim that the tyrant's act, appearances aside, is not of the same type as the case of drowning that he (Mill) mentioned, or allow that it is, but insist that it is morally right. He takes the first alternative. Does he have any principled view to defend? Or is this an *ad hoc* smokescreen? What does one do when the clergy puts you between Scylla and Charybdis?

In any case, the view he defends is seriously mistaken. Recall, Mill holds that the business of ethics is to tell us what acts are right. We should now add that under Mill's conception, ethical bankruptcy seems inevitable. The identification of acts – whether right or wrong – depends upon their intent, according to Mill's footnote. But if we contemplate what course of conduct we should take, that is, if we are faced with a choice and consider the various lines of action open to us in order to identify the right one, there is no existing set of intentions from which we can choose the right one. No test will sort the correct action from an empty set. Hence Mill's business must fail.

Where did Mill err? My guess: he stepped toward the cul-de-sac when he failed to distinguish the principle that evaluations of the merit of an act can be grounded independently of an appraisal of the agent who performed the act – something that is true – from the principle that evalua-tions of the merit of an act can be grounded independently of the moral evaluation of *any* agent – something that is false. It was, of course, just these principles that we saw the Aristotelian account kept distinct while Martineau seemingly failed to distinguish between them. For a closer look at them and how they can be separated and confused, let's turn now to Hume's moral thought. If my hunch is right, Mill thought the second principle true because the first is; Hume, on the other hand, seems to make the opposite mistake. He thinks the first principle is false because the second is.

VI

Hume and the Indirect View

———————◆———————

By our continual and earnest pursuit of a character, a name, a
reputation in the world, we bring our own deportment and
conduct frequently in review and consider how they appear in
the eyes of those who approach and regard us. This constant
habit of surveying ourselves, as it were in reflection, keeps alive
all the sentiments of right and wrong, and begets in noble
natures a certain reverence for themselves as well as others,
which is the surest guardian of every virtue. . . . here is
displayed the force of many sympathies. Our moral sentiment is
itself a feeling chiefly of that nature; and our regard to a
character with others seems to arise only from a care of
preserving a character with ourselves; and in order to attain this
end, we find it necessary to prop our tottering judgement on the
correspondent approbation of mankind.

Inquiry Concerning the Principles of Morals, 96–97

———————————————

Any conception of the moral point of view presupposes and
relies decisively upon a conception of virtue. And vice
versa. Such interdependence makes it possible to read a
philosopher's account of virtue as evidence for what he
takes the moral point of view to be. Or vice versa. To the
student of the history of ideas this is especially useful when
a writer, such as Sidgwick, discusses one of these topics –
in his case, the moral point of view – at great length, but
suppresses discussion of the other almost entirely. In the
case of David Hume, neither side of the picture is concealed; both the moral point of view and the nature of moral

virtues are treated explicitly and in great detail. The difficulty, if it is one, lies in the *apparent* fact that his views on
these two inseparable matters seem incommensurable. The
required linkage looks undone.

The aim of this and the next several chapters will be to
reconstruct a sufficient portion of Hume's moral theory to
reveal that his conception of human virtue is bifurcated;
that each of the two different conceptions of human virtue
rely decisively on a different conception of the moral point
of view; that these different points of view are each moral
points of view; that they are not reducible to some one
moral point of view without moral loss, since they correctly
characterize our moral situation. In pursuing this aim I
hope that a deeper understanding of the Indirect View, and
the relationship between moral principles and acts and
agents, and their evaluations, will emerge. In particular,
understanding Hume is crucial because his moral thought
provides a particularly deep theoretical account of the
double moral value that virtues such as friendship and generosity possess. Hence his theory of the interdependent nature of the right and the good, of which the double moral
value of friendship is merely one reflection, merits the most
serious attention. And not merely as a fascinating piece of
history.

Hume was one of the last moral philosophers of stature
to take virtues seriously: to regard a theory of virtues as
central to moral theory. Such a belief, shared by almost
every great moral thinker before him, was dispatched by
the Enlightenment; it is conspicuous by its absence in 19th
and 20th century moral philosophy. Most surprisingly, its
death went unnoticed. Why did it perish? I have yet to find
a convincing explanation. But I am sure that Hume was not
the assassin.

In this chapter we will be content to set the stage for
Hume's moral concerns. Our starting point for understanding Hume's theory of the virtues will be three claims about
his project. They are:

1   The central focus of Hume's moral theorizing, what an-
    imates it (to some extent, no doubt, because it gripped

him personally), is that a person must 'be able to bear his own survey.' (*T*, 626)[1]

2 Hume sought an account of 'the origin of morals.'

3 Hume takes the primary (or basic) objects of moral evaluation to be traits of character.

Let's examine each, keeping in mind that more amplification will be provided in due course.

(1) What does Hume mean by saying that a person must 'be able to bear his own survey'? Simply put, in the terminology of our day, we would say 'A person must have self-respect; he must be able to survey his life and conduct, and find that he merits a positive appraisal; that he is respect-worthy.'[2] A person must have a sense of his own existence as worthwhile. There is, as Hume says, 'nothing more useful to us in the conduct of life, than a due degree of pride, which makes us sensible of our own merit, and gives us a confidence and assurance in all our projects and enterprizes.' (*T*, 596–597)[3] 'A genuine and hearty pride, or self-esteem ... is essential to the character of a man of honour, and there is no quality of mind, which is more indispensably requisite to procure the esteem and approbation of mankind.' (*T*, 598)[4]

Hume's initial observation – an astute one, I think – is that we in fact survey our own conduct and life. That this is something in which we doggedly engage. Human life is full of effort and activity, work and play, joy and disappointment and anger and complacency, success and failure. We are creatures able to reflect on our triumphs and losses and everyday existence; we step back, as it were, and ask how things are going, whether we are successful, whether we could do better, whether the life being lived is worth living, worthwhile. Hume's genius is to notice that our tendency to survey our conduct and life systematically affects the quality and structure of our life, the life examined by ourself when we our spectators to ourself.

Hume, like Aristotle, thinks of a human life as a set of activities that can be viewed as constituting a performance that is good or bad, exemplary or disgusting, excellent or mediocre or average. The attitude formed by the assessment of the performance is self-respect. Possessing self-respect involves the conviction that one's character and life will be approved by anyone who will but assess it fairly. Hence self-respect supposes an implicit reference to shared standards of appraisal about what it is to be a good person living a good life. Since virtues or excellences just are the central constituents of living such a life, why Hume sees a theory of virtues as central to moral theory is straightforward. And since self-respect is the crowning attitude of self-recognition worn by the person who lives such a life, it is the modern secular, and more egalitarian, descendant of Aristotle's great-souled man (*megalopsuchos*).

Hume demands that people be able to survey themselves with satisfaction and respect. He needs, therefore, an account of how the survey should be conducted and what it seeks. Any systematic theory that attempts to show what qualities are estimable – which qualities provide grounds for respect – must rely on some conception of human nature. What are humans like? What potentialities do they possess that are worth developing? To be sure, Hume sees explicitly that his theory must study human nature and illuminate our psychological and sociological formation in order to show what materials are available, what their character is, and how they can or cannot be formed, reformed, and educated. In fact, Hume rightly sees that the demands of self-respect place restrictions on the *nature* of moral objects. How so?

A person's sense of self-respect refers implicitly to a set of evaluative standards; it is, for instance, the failure to meet such a standard, or, more precisely, the perception of failure, that causes a loss of self-respect. Such standards, let's say, are evaluative conceptions about the nature and ideals of right-living: they specify what is shameful, honorable, base, demeaning, odious, deplorable, decent, civil, only to be expected, disgraceful, et cetera. Such evaluative conceptions do not, and cannot, develop in a social vacuum. Our desire for self-respect – for a strong and positive sense of self-worth – and the fact that we take pleasure in self-respect, must be seen as a part of a complex network of social traits and characteristics. We praise and blame, criticize and eulogize; we admonish, berate, and scold; we applaud; we extol, laud, and glorify; we berate and denounce and censure and castigate; we sanction and advocate, we flatter and acclaim; we disparage, belittle, malign, and ridicule; we carp and cavil. We are the most unsolitary of creatures. Our evaluative conceptions about the nature and ideals of right-living are drawn from these networks of activities: models of conduct and character are established.[5] We *identify* with such models, taking them to be what we should be like, what we want to *be*. Our admiration and esteem for those whose character and conduct we approve and respect causes us to desire to become like them, to become the objects of such approval and respect.[6]

There are, then, systematic internal connections between a person's motivational structure and the evaluative conceptions that form the normative basis of his sense of self-respect through the identifications which he makes. A person is transformed by the social practices and roles in which he engages: his motivations, sentiments, and attitudes converge with those with whom he identifies;[7] the evaluative conceptions are internalized; a more developed and refined moral outlook emerges. By internalizing the norms and standards implicit in the roles, models and individuals with whom he identifies, by incorporating them into the normative basis of self-respect, a person's conception of himself changes and he with it.[8] The adoption of an evaluative conception carries with it a modification of the person's appraisals of himself and others in the light of the adopted standard; and doubly so, for he not only finds, say, certain activities to be deplorable, but also desires not to be the sort of person who would engage in such conduct. Those persons are worthy only of disparagement. So his attitudes and his feelings, his perspective on life, must be informed by the various models with which he identifies; what is enjoyed or regretted, what is found humiliating, shameful, honorable or vile cannot remain unchanged. His *identifications* are morally and psychologically transforming.

Hume is, I think, onto something pretty deep in trying to account for our moral sentiments by reference to our deep-felt need for recognition – for status and a confirmation of our life as being worthwhile. For that bespeaks recognition of the great fragility of the human ego.

(2) The second preliminary: Hume sought an account of the 'origin of morals.' In his terminology, he sought the *principles* of morality. Nothing less would establish him as the Newton of practical philosophy. But the meaning of the word 'principle' has changed since Hume's day; we have lost the strong sense in which 'principle' connoted 'origin, source, commencement, fundamental and ultimate quality.' But it is exactly that sense which Hume and his compatriots recognized and used. Locke, Berkeley, Butler, Pope, Mandeville, Hutcheson, Shaftesbury. Each used 'principles,' *inter alia*, to refer to the *springs of action* – a usage that is commonplace in the 17th and 18th century, and is tied to the historical origins of the term in *princeps* and *archē*, each commonly used to refer to the starting point of action. And such is Hume's usage: 'There are different ways of examining the Mind as well as the Body. One may consider it either as an Anatomist or as a Painter; either to discover its most secret Springs & Principles or to describe the Grace and Beauty of its Actions.'[9]

But 'principle' is not used to mean only 'origin.' It is also used, quite naturally, to refer to a fundamental quality: something that can explain other phenomena, but itself remains unexplained and unexplainable.[10] To inquire into the principles of morals is to inquire into the fundamental origins of character and conduct that explain the nature of our moral life, *as far as it can be explained*.

And, to inquire into the principles of morals as one would into natural philosophy – to follow Pope's dictum that we must 'Account for Moral, as for Nat'ral Things'[11] – would be to seek the *natural principles* of human nature that explain our moral life:

> Yes, Nature's road must ever be prefer'd;
> Reason here is no guide, but still a guard;
> 'Tis hers to rectify, not overthrow,
> And treat this passion more as friend than foe:

A mightier Pow'r the strong direction sends,
And sev'ral Men impels to sev'ral ends.
Like varying winds, by other passions tost,
This drives them constant to a certain coast.
Let pow'r or knowledge, gold or glory, please,
Or (oft more strong than all) the love of ease;
Thro' life 'tis followed, ev'n at life's expence;
The merchant's toil, the sage's indolence,
The monk's humility, the hero's pride,
All, all alike, find Reason on their side.

    Th' Eternal Art educing good from ill,
Grafts on this Passion our best principle:
'Tis thus the Mercury of Man is fix'd,
Strong grows the Virtue with his nature mix'd;
The dross cements what else were too refin'd,
And in one interest body acts with mind.

    As fruits ungrateful to the planter's care
On savage stocks inserted learn to bear;
The surest Virtues thus from Passions shoot,
Wild Nature's vigor working at the root.
What crops of wit and honesty appear
From spleen, from obstinacy, hate, or fear!
See anger, zeal and fortitude supply;
Ev'n av'rice, prudence; sloth, philosophy;
Lust, thro' some certain strainers well refin'd,
Is gentle love, and charms all womankind:
Envy, to which the ignoble mind's a slave,
Is emulation in the learn'd or brave:
Nor Virtue, male or female, can we name,
But what will grow on Pride, or grow on Shame.
            (*Ep.* 2, 162–195)

The pattern of such naturalistic explanations was that thought to have been employed so successfully by Newton: the analysis of the complex (to be explained) into the simple element or qualities from which the complex could be synthesized. The general pattern for explaining any phenomenon *naturally* was to account for *it* in terms of something more basic: the elemental or *original* qualities of that produced it. Hence any complete natural explanation required the specification of the causal genesis of the object of explanation in terms of fundamental qualities or principles. It follows that any phenomenon must be *either* susceptible to natural explanation *or* an *original* quality, because *no original quality is explainable.* As Hume observed, 'we can give no reason for our most general and most refined principles, beside our experience of their reality ... this impossibility of explaining ultimate principles ... 'tis a defect common to ... all the sciences ...' (*T*, xxii)[12]

That Hume wanted to place moral thought on the same sound footing recently achieved in natural philosophy is not at doubt:

> But 'tis at least worth while to try of the science of *man* will not admit of the same accuracy which several parts of natural philosophy are found susceptible of. There seems to be all the reason in the world to imagine that it may be carried to the greatest degree of exactness. If, in examining several phaenomena, we find that they resolve themselves into one common principle, and can trace this principle into another, we shall at last arrive at those simple principles, on which all the rest depend. And tho' we can never arrive at the ultimate principles, 'tis a satisfaction to go as far as our faculties will allow us.[13]

Moral distinctions and qualities were to be explained through a small number of fundamental qualities or principles that generated them;[14] moral distinctions and qualities that characterize our moral life were to moral philosophy what the movement of the planets and other objects were to natural philosophy; and Hume was to be to the former what Newton was to the latter.

Hume's naturalized account of what qualities are estimable and why they are so is enormously complex. Undoubtedly, there are a number of different ways we could divide it to facilitate its consideration. One such division, which it is useful to mark for analytical purposes, is the separation of the account of which qualities are estimable and why, from the account of the facts about observing which qualities are estimable. The latter account deals primarily with how people engaged in moral evaluation might disagree or get the wrong results because of factors that often influence the evaluation, but should not; and, of course, the extent to which such disagreements can be reconciled, and a common standard of evaluation established:

> When a man denominates another his *enemy*, his *rival*, his *antagonist*, his *adversary*, he is understood to speak the language of self-love and to express sentiments peculiar to himself and arising from his particular circumstances and situation. But when he bestows on any other man the epithets of *vicious* or *odious* or *depraved*, he then speaks another language and expresses sentiments in which he expects all his audience are to concur with him. He must here, therefore, depart from his private and particular situation and must choose a point of view common to him with others. (*I*, 93)

Hume's account of moral evaluation here parallels his account of aesthetic evaluation, his theory of taste. In each the sign of a sound evaluation is that it expresses what he calls *durable* admiration for its object.[15] It is durable because it is not peculiar to oneself, one's time, one's circumstances; rather it is shareable and sustainable. What makes evaluations possess or lack such a quality is what I shall call Hume's model of the 'Judicious Critic.'[16] The Judicious Critic represents Hume's account of the mechanism of discrimination and identification employed in sound moral judgement. The Judicious Critic is the creature who, when engaged in moral evaluation, gets all the relevant facts and features into view, and does whatever is necessary for a proper discernment of the object of evaluation; then, and only then, is the moral sense evoked in him.

Enough said, for the present. We shall return to look at some of the features of this critic's judiciousness in examining Hume's theory of the virtues.

(3) The third, and last, preliminary is the most straightforward and noncontroversial. It is simply that Hume takes the primary objects of moral judgements to be traits of character: ''Tis evident, that when we praise any actions, we regard only the motives that produced them, and consider the actions as signs or indications of certain principles

in the mind and temper. The external performance has no merit. We must look within to find the moral quality.' $(T, 477)$[17] Why Hume thought this is something I hope to explain; for that explanation will reveal his ties of allegiance to the Indirect View, and cast some light on our previous discussion of Price, Reid, and Mill.

VII

The Dualism of Humean Virtues

———————◆———————

Actions are not virtuous nor vicious; but only so far as they are
proofs of certain Qualitys or durable Principles in the Mind.
This is a Point I shou'd have establish'd more expressly than I
have done ... tis on the Goodness or Badness of the Motives
that the Virtue of the Action depends. This proves, that to
every virtuous actions there must be a Motive or impelling
Passion distinct from the Virtue, & that Virtue can never be the
sole Motive to any Action. You do not assent to this; tho' I
think there is no Proposition more certain or important.

David Hume in a letter to Francis Hutcheson, September 1739

———————————————

Book III of Hume's *Treatise* commences with an argument
to establish, first, that moral distinctions are not derived
from reason, and second, that, instead, they are derived
from our moral sense. Such is the task of the first two
sections of Book III. Upon satisfying himself that these
goals have been attained, Hume asks his readers whether he
has successfully uncovered the origin of morals – the ultimate source and cause of moral good and evil – in the
process:

> It may now be ask'd *in general*, concerning this pain or
> pleasure that distinguishes moral good and evil, *From what
> principle is it derived, and when does it arise in the human
> mind?* To this I reply, *first*, that 'tis absurd to imagine, that in
> every particular instance, these sentiments are produced by an
> *original* quality and *primary* constitution. For as the number
> of our duties is, in a manner, infinite, 'tis impossible that our

original instincts should extend to each of them, and from our
very first infancy impress upon the human mind all that
multitude of precepts, which are contained in the compleatest
system of ethics ... 'Tis necessary, therefore, to find some
more general principles, upon which all our notions of morals
are founded. (*T*, 473)

Hume's science of virtue and vice, therefore, is not completed by the discovery and documentation of the fact that
all moral judgements concerning virtue and vice are
grounded in moral sentiments that would be aroused in a
Judicious Critic. Why we respond favorably (or unfavor-
ably), and hence why certain qualities are virtues (or vices),
admits of further explanation. Indeed, further explanation
is required. Otherwise, Hume would be compelled to assert
that each virtue is grounded in an original instinct: something that admits of no further explanation and is merely
discovered empirically. Since a multitude of virtues and
vices exists, and Hume is committed to a methodological
thesis that 'a few principles produce all the variety we observe in the universe' (*T*,473),[1] he concludes that the principles of morality have not yet been revealed. The direction
of inquiry, however, has been fixed:

... we are still brought back to our first position, that virtue
is distinguished by the pleasure, and vice by the pain that any
action, sentiment, or character gives us by the mere view and
contemplation. This decision is very commodius; because it
reduces us to this simple question, *Why any action or
sentiment, upon the general view or survey, gives a certain
satisfaction or uneasiness,* in order to shew the origin of its
moral rectitude or depravity, without looking for any
incomprehensible relations and qualities, which never did
exist in nature, nor even in our imagination, by any clear and
distinct conception. I flatter myself I have executed a great
part of my present design by a state of the question which
appears to me so free from ambiguity and obscurity. (*T*, 475–
476)[2]

In what will the further explanation of our moral sentiments consist? Hume immediately hints at the answer: it

may be due to the fact that 'our sense of some virtues is artificial, and that of others natural.' (*T*, 475) To be sure, the hint hardly seems necessary. The remainder of the *Treatise* is concerned with only two topics: the artificial virtues and the natural virtues. Our sense of artificial virtue is explained further in great detail; for some of the natural virtues some additional explanation concerning our moral sentiments is provided. For some, however, no further explanation will be forthcoming:

> Moral good and evil are certainly distinguished by our *sentiments*, not by *reason*: But these sentiments may arise either from the mere species or appearance of characters and passions, or from reflexions on their tendency to the happiness of mankind, and of particular persons. My opinion is that both these causes are intermix'd in our judgements of morals ... There are, however, instances ... wherein this immediate taste or sentiment produces our approbation. Wit and a certain easy and disengag'd behavior, are qualities *immediately agreeable* to others, and command their love and esteem. Some of these qualities produce satisfaction in others by particular *original* principles of human nature, which cannot be accounted for: Others may be resolved into principles which are more general. (*T*, 589–590)

Exactly how does Hume's distinction between natural and artificial virtues, and his discussion of each, enable him to provide some further explanation of our moral sentiments, of our moral sense? In several ways, to which we must now turn our attention.

Hobbes' writings forced moralists once again to address the perennial question of what is natural and what is artificial. Is property natural or artificial? And justice? The state? The desire for someone else's happiness? Hobbes boldly partitioned the natural and the artificial, letting the former categorize facts about life in the state of nature, where men have no other law than their own appetites, the latter facts about life in a commonwealth introduced to escape the nasty character of the state of nature. He thereby rescued human nature from the role consigned to it by the Protestant Reformation: namely, that of being wholly corrupt and irrelevant to the foundation of morality. The moral laws, the laws of nature, must be grounded in our nature and connect with facts about us: what we want and fear. Man is naturally uncivil, but is civilized by fear.

Hume's discussion of the natural and artificial is applied to virtues: virtues are of two sorts, artificial and natural. What explains the difference, as we will see, is an underlying distinction between passions and sentiments that are natural, as contrasted with artificial. It is with this underlying distinction that we should begin.

Which passions are natural? Which artificial? Hume's answer is, I think, ingenious. To understand it, we should distinguish two different senses in which a passion could be said to be natural: a distinction that Hume makes nowhere explicitly, but is required to make sense of his thought. Hume's task is to explain, as far as one can, the origin of our moral sense, our moral sentiments. Such an account of the genesis of our moral sentiments can be divided roughly into two parts: first, what are the primitive materials from which mature moral sensibilities grow? Second, how is this product produced? How are the mature moral sentiments formed and developed? Hume answers the first question by requiring that all sentiments be explained, ultimately, only by reference to other sentiments or psychological principles governing them, the chief principles of this sort being custom and sympathy. Tentatively, let's call a passion *natural* if it plays an explanatory role in the account of other sentiments, but is not itself susceptible to such an explanatory account. Calling a passion natural, then, locates its role in an explanatory system of the passions. But since its role is a special one – that of an unexplained explainer which must be empirically ascertained – it also locates it as a fundamental quality of creatures like us, a basic endowment of human nature, if you will.

So much, so good. There is, however, a rub. If we take Hume seriously, we must admit that we are *never* in a position to apprehend any natural passion, in this sense, in its natural state: that is, *as natural*. Why not? Because all passions are identified in some social milieu; any sentiment or passion relies essentially on a social fabric and is inseparable from it; what sentiment it is and how it is to be understood is not determinable independently from its social backdrop. As Hume says so pithily: 'We can form no wish that has no reference to society ... Whatever other passions may be actuated by; pride, ambition, avarice, curiosity, revenge or lust; the soul or animating principle of them all is sympathy; nor wou'd they have any force, were we to abstract entirely from the thought and feelings of others.' (*T*, 363)[3]

Hume's idea that all sentiments have reference to society, to an implicit 'intercourse of sentiments,' might best be captured by the thought that all passions contain a consciousness of others, of social values and standards that have been learned. Compare, for instance, the unselfconscious manner in which a four month old infant looks about the room – absolutely no evident awareness of social demands, of others as anything but interesting pieces of world furniture – with the already self-conscious manner in which, say, the nine month old child expresses a consciousness of others, a desire to please them. In the latter case there is no *irreflective* manner any longer. And so it is with our sentiments and passions, being molded as they are by sympathy, Hume's psychological principle of passion contagion and communication:

> No quality of human nature is more remarkable, both in itself and in its consequences, than that propensity we have to sympathize with others, and to receive by communication their inclinations and sentiments, however different from, or even contrary to our own. This is not only conspicuous in children, who implicitly embrace every opinion propos'd to them; but also in men of the greatest judgement and understanding, who find it very difficult to follow their own reason or inclination, in opposition to that of their friends and daily companions. To this principle we ought to ascribe the great uniformity we may observe in the humours and turn of thinking of those of the same nation ... Hatred, resentment, esteem, love, courage, mirth, melancholy; all these passions I *feel more from communication than from my own natural temper and disposition.*[4]

Since 'the minds of men are mirrors to one another ... reflect[ing] each others emotions' (*T*, 365), opinions and sentiments of our own must be 'seconded by the opinions and sentiments of others' (*T*, 316); otherwise they will not be durable, they will not persist. Thus *all* passions and sentiments, on Hume's analysis, require a social milieu of 'reassurance' and 'secondary' support: they are the result of many sympathies. The 'intercourse of sentiments' (*T*, 603) produced by sympathy makes possible conversation about sentiments and matters of taste.[5] Individuals and their passions are products of social experience; philosophical individualism of any sort is misguided because society, not man, is the basic natural unit: 'But tho' it be possible for men to maintain a small uncultivated society without government, 'tis impossible they shou'd maintain a society of any kind without justice.' (*T*, 541)[6]

Our experience is social in nature in the first instance; the objects of moral experience – persons, actions, states of affairs – are social objects. Our moral conceptions must be understood as part of a total culture and history. They are not intelligible without some reference, implicit or explicit, to the conception and experiences of other members of the social order.[7] This fact is the crucial premise in Hume's rejection of the philosophical individualism of an anthropology shared by Hobbes and Locke: the idea that society is, *au fond*, a set of individuals; that they are primordials; that societies are formed by these individuals as compounds are formed by atoms.

It is not just that we happen to be social creatures, though, in fact, we are.[8] Social practices and institutions are not the intended product of deliberate action undertaken by a set of individuals, nor can the social order be comprehended adequately as an end result of the action of such independent pre-social individuals: they are mythical creatures, fabrications which can be understood only by implicitly presupposing the existence of what they try to explain. Habits, customs, expectations, traditions: these are things that create social regularities constitutive of the social order,[9] making possible social experiences within the order, experiences structured by those habits, customs, or ways of life. The emergence of public institutions like the system of exchange and the laws governing property, institutions whose *very evolution* is based in the realities of human nature and everyday life, are splendid examples of creations that cannot be matched by our rational capacities. Such institutions are not the product of rational construction and could not be brought about by an attempt to implement such a construction if it could be anticipated.

Were Hume alive today, his voice would be familiar and comforting. For his thought is that the moral sense is like other senses: they are naturally occurring instruments of detection that are never seen *au naturel*, but instead, always clothed in the effects of enculturation and history. Each must, nevertheless, be given a naturalistic account. The student of human behavior will notice that there are patterns of, say, simplicity, relevance, and similarity in which human observers generally concur; he will hypothesize that such patterns reflect our nature as expressed in culturally based judgement. Such patterns, then, are not explainable without recognition that they are partly the projections of the feelings and beliefs of the spectators; just as are the patterns that inform our recognition of beauty and virtue. The student of human nature, in both natural and practical philosophy, has as his task the specification of the theory – the psychological processes – that will permit us to explain the senses, moral or nonmoral, and thereby understand the patterns.

How does this description, of the role that sympathy and custom play in passion formation, affect the tentative account of the (first) sense in which passions or sentiments are said to be natural? Well, passions that are natural (in the first sense) must be identified in some social medium that conceals, to some extent, their natural form. What is their *natural* form? It would be what they are like in the absence of the effects of custom and sympathy. Very little, then, can be said about such natural passions: only that they provide boundaries or limits to what can be made of creatures like us through education and artifice, through the effects of custom and sympathy.[10] We are not, as Hume pointedly remarks when considering Mandeville's *Fable*, infinitely malleable, utterly plastic.[11]

Passions that are natural in the first sense are, qua natural, hypothesized entities that help us to explain and understand other passions, both natural and artificial. (And hence natural and artificial virtues.) Hence there must be a second sense in which a passion or sentiment is said to be natural, one which severs the connection between a passion being *natural* and being *original*.[12] For passions that are natural (in the first sense) are original; therefore, they cannot be explained by other natural passions.

What is meant by calling a passion 'natural' in the second sense? That it is not artificial; that its *object* is 'of a kind that cou'd be pursu'd by the natural and inartificial passions of men.' (*T*, 497)[13] Calling a passion *natural* marks it as being of the kind that can fund a natural virtue; but 'our sense of every kind of virtue is not natural ... [since] there are some virtues, that produce pleasure and approbation by means of an artifice or contrivance, which arises from the circumstances and necessity of mankind.' (*T*, 477) Such artificial virtues, of which Hume takes justice to be the most important, are the *result* of conventions that channel and educate the natural sentiments,[14] creating sentiments such as an esteem for justice and an abhorrence of injustice.[15] Hence the terms 'natural' and 'artificial' cannot be understood without reference to Hume's official account of the moral sense: the feeling of approval or disapproval aroused in a Judicious Critic. Each kind of principle produces satisfaction (or dissatisfaction) in the Judicious Critic for different reasons: the approval aroused by the contemplation of principles that are natural is explainable by the effects of sympathy, custom, and the ideas that certain things are immediately agreeable to other people or to a person himself without any further consideration; the approval aroused by the contemplation of artificial principles is explainable by the effects of sympathy, custom, natural sentiments, and the idea (made possible by sympathy) that certain things are agreeable because they advance the public good or interest, the good of society, of mankind: something that is conventionally constructed, that is constituted by artifice.[16]

To understand Hume's distinction better, consider why he takes justice to be an artificial virtue. Hume contends that justice must be understood to be artificial because there is no natural motive to be just. Why is the issue of a motive relevant? Because 'all virtuous actions derive their merit from virtuous motives.' (*T*, 478) 'When we praise any actions,' Hume says, 'we regard only the motives that produced them, and consider the actions as signs or indications of certain principles in the mind and temper. The external performance has no merit. We must look within to find the moral quality ... the ultimate object of our praise and approbation is the motive ...' (*T*, 477)[17] From this principle it follows that regard for the virtue of the act cannot be what bestows merit on the act. Suppose, however, for the sake of argument, it did. Regard for the virtue of the act requires the act be seen as virtuous because of its virtuous motive. But if regard for the virtue of the act bestows merit on the act, then *it* must be the virtuous motive which it sees as making the act virtuous: something Hume takes to be absurd, since the virtuous motive that makes the act virtuous must exist antecedent to our recognition of the virtue.[18] Therefore, it is 'an undoubted maxim *that no action can be virtuous, or morally good, unless there be in human nature some motive to produce it distinct from its sense of morality.*' (*T*, 479)

If we grant Hume his principle that the virtue of virtuous acts must be due to their relation to the motive that produced them – or modify it a bit, as I would prefer, to claim only that the virtue is due to their relation to a character of a certain type – Hume's argument is certainly a good one. For consider any such virtuous motive. It leads people to act in ways that we morally approve. Suppose, though, we thought that such a motive was grounded in a judgement concerning the virtue of the act: as we might put it, that, say, this act is to be done because it is a duty or morally required. But this second judgement – that the act is a duty or morally required – must be understood in light of the principle we granted. That it is a duty, then, is a judgement grounded in a judgement like: this act is to be done because it is what a person of 'morally approbative' character would do, which judgement is itself grounded facts about characters of this type, especially their characteristic motivations. Hence it would be circular and vacuous to say that such characters were moved to act in such ways by the thought that it was their duty to do so. The sense of virtue cannot be self-grounding.

Artificial virtues, such as justice, must be recognized as artificial because they fail to satisfy the undoubted maxim that has been deduced: they are related to actions to which the sense of duty is attached, yet for which there does not seem to be the requisite prior natural motive (that renders the act meritorious):

> .. suppose a person to have lent me a sum of money ... *What reason or motive do I have to restore the money?* It will, perhaps, be said, that my regard to justice and abhorrence of villainy and knavery, are sufficient reason for me, if I have the least grain of honesty, or sense of duty and obligation. And this answer, no doubt, is just and satisfactory to a man in his civiliz'd state, and when train'd up according to a certain discipline and education. But in his rude and more *natural* condition, if you are pleas'd to call such a condition natural, this answer would be rejected as perfectly unintelligible and sophisticated. (*T*, 479)[19]

Since we regard such acts as required by justice, and regard justice as a virtue, a chronicle of (i) how and why we have any motive to perform such acts is needed, as well as an account of (ii) how and why justice is a virtue. The explanation of the latter will, of course, be different from that which accounts for any natural virtue. Hume needs to address each of these issues. And he does. The conclusion of the *Treatise*, Parts II and III of Book III, is directed to just these topics. First we get Hume's explanation of why each of us has a motive or reason for entering the conventions of justice that provide for stability of the possession of goods;[20] next we get his explanation of why justice is regarded as a virtue;[21] finally, Hume turns to his account of the origin of natural virtues.[22]

A distinction between natural and artificial virtues such as Hume draws, whatever its merits in his theory, has certain reflexive implications that he does not notice. The distinction purports to distinguish virtues associated with natural motives from virtues associated with artificial motives. Hume takes as evidence for the correctness of this manner of sorting motives the fact that we do automatically and unselfconsciously treat some motives as natural, while hesitating or refusing to treat others similarly. Fair enough. This is one way – indeed, a profound one – that we order our experiences and understand ourselves. However, we cannot, in examining our nature, dissociate ourselves altogether from what is under scrutiny. Our inclination, and Hume's, to agree with such evidence is *itself* the reflection of classifications based upon socially formed attitudes and beliefs of the *very type being classified*. So one who uses the distinction reveals the degree and nature of his enculturation by the weight he attaches to its ability to sweep the natural from the artificial. It locates one's place in the labyrinth; it does *not* permit one to climb to some fabled neutral perspective – out of the cave, so to speak.

I take this manner of identifying the natural and artificial to be an especially important and intriguing fact not merely because of what it reveals about Hume, but because of what it reveals about us. We also believe that a sound conception and practice of justice requires that the virtue of justice be swept away from our natural character in certain ways. There is, however, something of a paradox here. Justice depends upon the character of the persons it serves, and it also conflicts with it. Or so I shall argue. It is to the details of this conflict, as revealed in Hume's thought, that we must now turn.

VIII

Moral Points of View

———————◆———————

Men are now cured of their passion for hypotheses and systems
in natural philosophy, and will hearken to no argument but
those derived from experience. It is full time they should
attempt a like reformation in all moral disquisitions and reject
every system of ethics, however subtle or ingenious, which is
not founded on fact and observation.

Inquiry Concerning the Principles of Morals, 8

———————————————————

In something of an exaggeration Hume claims that 'the only
difference betwixt the natural virtues and justice lies in this,
that the good, which results from the former, arises from
every single act, and is the object of some natural passion:
Whereas a single act of justice, consider'd in itself, may
often be contrary to the public good; and 'tis only the con-
currence of mankind in a general scheme or system of
action, which is advantageous.' (*T*, 579) Besides the now
familiar point that the individual acts of justice may not, by
themselves, promote the end by which the rules of justice
(that dictate those acts be performed) are justified,[1] Hume
is implicitly claiming, or at least committed to the assertion,
that the two sorts of virtue can conflict. How is this possible?

> When I relieve persons in distress, my natural humanity is
> my motive; and so far as my succour extends, so far I have
> promoted the happiness of my fellow-creatures. But if we
> examine all the questions, that come before any tribunal of
> justice, we shall find, that, considering each case apart, it
> wou'd as often be an instance of humanity to decide contrary
> to the laws of justice as conformable to them. Judges take

82

from the poor to give to the rich; they bestow on the
dissolute the labour of the industrious; and put into the hands
of the vicious the means of harming both themselves and
others. (*T*, 579)

This discord – here, between justice and a natural virtue,
benevolence, and more generally, between the natural and
artificial virtues – is a product of a clash between the two
differing conceptions of a moral point of view that each
presupposes. Hume is explicitly aware of the potential for
variance between the two sorts of virtues; he is not, I think,
sufficiently attuned to its sources or significance.

Let's supply an initial gloss of the differing conceptions
of the moral point of view that each of the different sorts of
virtues presupposes. We can amplify, extend, and qualify
such a description shortly, as proves necessary when docu-
menting Hume's commitment to the differing conceptions.

Consider, first, the artificial virtues, of which Hume takes
justice to be a paradigm. (When Hume talks about justice
he is primarily concerned with the rules of property, with
civil rather than *criminal* law.[2]) Hume was a member of the
Scottish Enlightenment; he, like his fellow travelers, was
expressly concerned with the economic advancement of
Scotland. Hume threw his hat in the rapidly growing ring
of thinkers who understood that the stability of common-
wealths and the opportunities that they afforded for the
development of culture, of the arts and science, turned cru-
cially on the role of the economy.[3] He was deeply committed to making commerce and culture flourish – as, of course,
were most 18th century Scottish men of letters. Especially
the former, if only because it was seen as a prerequisite for
the enhancement of the latter: 'The greatness of a state, and
the happiness of its subjects, how independent soever they
may be supposed to be in some respects, are commonly
allowed to be inseparable with regard to commerce; and as
private men receive greater security, in the possession of
their trade and riches, from the power of the public, so the
public becomes powerful in proportion to the opulence and
extensive commerce of private men.'[4]
His thought on property and justice reveals these inter-

ests. The purpose of government is seen as securing the conditions necessary for economic progress: to provide the rule of law governing property necessary for the economic progress, obtained through commerce and industry, that will make possible the good life. Hume's addition to Hobbes' thought is that the economic sector of the social order is a most, perhaps the most, decisive factor in determining the good life. The artificial virtue of justice comes clothed in a juridical attire: it displays a model of moral relationships that is best called a 'rights' model, a contractual model generated, I think, by seeing a key dimension of our moral lives as a moral commerce with others governed by the laws of contract that make commerce possible. How so?

Ask yourself about those people with whom you think you stand, or can stand, in some moral relationship: what is it about them that makes you bear this relationship to them? The 'rights' model answers by claiming that the most fundamental relationships that characterize a community of moral agents are contractual relationships among free and equal partners about whom you, as a participant in moral commerce, need know nothing else about save that they are partners as well. Imagine, for a moment, that the social order is composed of a set of guilds or trading companies to which all persons are members. What is needed, to prevent serious inconveniences in the marketplace of life, and to allow these economic organizations and their members to pursue their business in a reasonable manner, are the rules of contract establishing the rights, privileges, and obligations of various members of the social order. Without such rules, social and economic progress will be thwarted. Hence moral commerce is held inseparable from commerce among anonymous players in the economic marketplace, and is modeled after it.

But how are such rules to be constructed? Answer: from the point of view of *anyone*, since only then will each person – each free man, each equal partner to the social contract – have a reason to agree to the rules. Hence the moral point of view presupposed by this conception is ruthlessly legalistic: under it, all persons lose their particularity, any feature about them that distinguishes them from anyone else (and hence might provide a basis for some favourable treatment for them, a treatment not sustainable from the point of view of anyone, but only those so favored). The rule of law must fix considerations 'as may be equal to every member of society' to secure the expectation by members of impartial treatment from magistrates, treatment that 'remove[s] everything arbitrary and partial from the decision of property.'[5] The rules of justice, therefore, look only at a typical universal person. In that way alone will the system of rules be able to secure a reason for anyone to agree to the rules:

> Every man's interest is peculiar to himself, and the aversions and dislikes which result from it cannot be supposed to affect others in like degree ... The intercourse of sentiments, therefore, in society and conversation makes us form some general unalterable standard by which we may approve or disapprove of characters and manners. And though the *heart takes part not entirely with those general notions*, nor regulates all its love and hatred by the *universal, abstract differences* of vice and virtue *without regard to self or the persons with whom we are more intimately connected*, yet these moral differences have a considerable influence ...[6]

Failure to assume the perspective of *anyone* – say, for example, as when we look at a person as our *friend*, or *sister*, or *daughter* – causes us to entertain considerations irrelevant to the rules of justice. *Who* you are counts for nothing; you enter into the count only by being one more source of interest – a source *just like* any other[7] – from which the end that justifies the rules of justice is calculated. Which is to say that the moral point of view presupposed by the Humean artificial virtues is distinguished by its impartiality of abstraction: it is indifferent to any specific relations between individual people because it does not recognize them. It refuses to countenance any 'consideration [about] the characters, situations, and connections' of individual persons even though such a refusal results, at times, in preventable evils.[8] It is, then, a view that many regard as distinctively Kantian in outlook,[9] though its historical source is undoubtedly the Stoic conception of morality grounded in eternal natural laws. Its striking characteristic is its emphatic denunciation of the relevance of a person's identity to moral thought; it is at home in a community of strangers because the law of contract, moral and nonmoral, must be constructed to govern conduct and relationships among strangers, while providing each with a reason to obey it. Or so *it* claims.

Such a partiality for the impersonal is not fully compatible with the natural virtues and the moral point of view they presuppose. Consider, for example, a father's care for his children.[10] The father's natural affection and love binds him to his children; he cares for them and seeks their well-being because they are his children. This familiar personal relationship between the father and children is central to our understanding of his actions as an expression of natural virtue. His acts have as their object the good of *his* children; they are done because of his love and affection *for them*. But just as 'there is no such passion in human minds, as the love of mankind, merely as such, *independent of personal qualities, or services, or relations to ourself*,'[11] so there is no universal parental love and affection. The thought that his children are no different from, nor any more valuable or important than any other children, is farcical and outrageous from this point of view: the whimsical and bizarre creation of some misguided moral enthusiast. Which is to say that the moral point of view presupposed by the natural virtues is distinct from and may, at times, conflict with the moral point of view presupposed by the artificial virtues. Each recognizes a different set of considerations as morally relevant and irrelevant.

Since artificial virtues, such as justice, depend upon the character of the persons in whom they are inculcated, it is a bit of a puzzle that the natural and artificial virtues can and do conflict. What better expresses the character of persons than the natural passions? Indeed, Hume seems to affirm just that and more. He, like Butler, who he much admired, professes that the virtuousness of an act must be grounded in the naturalness of the passion that gives rise to it:[12]

since no action can be laudable or blameable, without some
motives or impelling passions, distinct from the sense of
morals, these distinct passions must have a great influence on
that sense. 'Tis according to their general force in human
nature, that we praise or blame. In judging the beauty of
animal bodies, we always carry in our eye the oeconomy of a
certain species; and where the limbs and features observe that
proportion, which is common to the species, we pronounce
them handsome and beautiful. In like manner we always
consider the *natural* and *usual* force of the passions, when we
determine concerning vice and virtue; and if the passions
depart very much from the common measures on either side,
they are always disapproved as vicious. A man naturally loves
his children better than his nephews, his nephews better than
his cousins, his cousins better than strangers, when
everything else is equal. Hence arise our common measures of
duty, in preferring the one to the other. Our sense of duty
always follows the common and natural course of our
passions.[13]

Hume takes this partiality of natural affections and
passions to place limits on moral thought because it can
only be modified and extended; it can be remedied and
provided a more edifying patina, but not excluded. The
character of persons who engage in moral thought places
limits on the character of the thought. How and why does
he arrive at this conclusion?

The very naturalness of personal affections that 'has the
greatest influence on the moral sense' must be respected;
but, its partiality must be subdued, says Hume. How both
are possible is a tad puzzling. Nonetheless, subdued the
natural affections must be if justice is to exist. For 'in the
original frame of mind, our strongest attention is confin'd
to ourselves,' and our limited generosity in a condition of
scarce goods,[14] leads to results damaging to our interests in
the absence of conventions guaranteeing stability of possession. So we need the rules of justice, and we obtain them
only through sympathy. It is the workhorse that enlarges
and extends our natural partiality to create a sense of justice
which, once created through artifice and convention, and

based in some natural motive, is just as natural as any natural sentiment.[15] Through the principle of sympathy the emotions, sentiments, and affections of others are communicated 'as in strings equally wound up' (*T*, 576) and 'reverberating' from person to person (*T*, 365); sympathy takes us 'so far out of our selves, as to give the same pleasure or uneasiness in the character of others, as if they had a tendency to our own advantage or loss.' (*T*, 579) It is through it that our interest extends to the public good, to which we would otherwise be indifferent.

Hume's account of the natural and the artificial, and their interrelationship, creates a vertigo, does it not? The heady purpose of the account is to provide a theory that will permit us to explain our moral sense, our moral sentiments. But, as the reconstruction had disclosed, Hume thinks (i) that our nature, as revealed by the naturalness of our passions and our partiality for those close to us, erects impenetrable boundaries for the refinement of our moral sentiments; (ii) that the artificial virtues are, and *must* be created from natural passions; and, (iii) that the artificial virtues provide a remedy in moral judgement and understanding, through education and convention, for the very partiality that they must respect *and yet* at the same time necessitates them. The key, then, to an unexpurgated understanding of Hume's account of the moral sentiments lies in digesting how moral sentiments build on themselves.

Hume always saw as his goal the establishment of a science of morality without the aid of revelation, with no appeal to divine purpose or design, and no aspect of morality subject to divine underwriting; instead, morality must be grounded in human nature, in the natural order of things. Understanding Hume's moral thought requires the fullest appreciation of this point. There can be no hidden conception of God or divine purpose in a proper account of our moral sense, of our moral nature. Human life has no *telos*, no proper end or function, guaranteed by biology (as Aristotle maintained) or through God's benevolence and providence, as modern Christians maintained. There is no such externally guaranteed purpose by which human life can be understood and by reference to which a kind of human life can be justified. Rather, all justification is internal to the human condition.[16] There is no God *or metaphysical substitute* – for example, the conception of reason employed by Locke in his *Second Treatise* – to which appeal can be made.

Hume found that among the contemporaries he admired most, Butler and Hutcheson, the new experimental approach, used so successfully in natural philosophy by Newton, was not wholly secular. Instead, it was utilized in an examination of human nature to reveal and confirm man's purpose: i.e., God's purpose for man. Thus Hume complained to Hutcheson that 'I cannot agree to your sense of *Natural*. Tis founded on final causes; which is a consideration that appears to me pretty uncertain & unphilosophical. For pray, what is the End of Man? Is he created for Happiness or for Virtue?'[17]

In a later letter the same complaint was focused by reference to Butler's work:

> You seem ... to embrace Dr. Butler's Opinion in his
> Sermons on human Nature; that our moral Sense has an
> Authority distinct from its Force and Durableness, & that
> because we always think it *ought* to prevail. But this is
> nothing but an Instinct or Principle, which approves of itself
> upon reflection; and that is common to all of them.[18]

Hume's point is that there is no hierarchical structure of human powers and principles, there is no Butlerian pyramid with conscience or the moral sense *ordering* and *governing* other particular and general passions. This view of our internal structure as a system of various parts, organized by principles of moral government, a sort of internal great chain of being, is grounded in a final cause – that this order of our psyche is brought about by the deliberate construction of some mind – and, in any case, is not true to the facts. What order and stability is found in the soul and in society arises insensibly and by degree;[19] and can be accounted for only by our sense of the natural and its interplay with custom and convention. There is no further order or purpose to things.[20] There is no further explanation.

The moral sentiments, then, must be explained without any appeal to the supernatural order of things. They must be 'account'd for as things natur'l.' And, if we take Hume at his word that we cannot depart very much from the 'natural and usual' force of the passions, and that 'our first and most natural sentiment of morals is founded on the nature of our passions' (*T*, 491), it is clear that the natural virtues must retain their moral force and integrity even while the artificial virtues acquire theirs.[21] But since the two sorts of virtues can clash, it follows that no unified account of the moral sense can be given. Hence the dual account Hume provides in Book III.

Many students of Hume's thought will, no doubt, find this conclusion troubling. One reason it discomforts many modern thinkers is that it conflicts with deeply held moral beliefs. For if we import the principle that any conception of virtue presupposes and relies on a moral point of view, we can quickly infer that Hume is committed to there being two different and not fully compatible moral points of view: that is, there is no unified moral point of view from which all moral conflicts and issues are resolvable. Of course, this is what Hume says, more or less. To be sure, he does not claim, as modern thinkers do, that moral points of view are perspectives for conflict resolution. But he does think there is no harmonious, unitary account of morality, of our moral sense, of our moral sentiments. Nor does he think there *needs* to be one. This last thought – that there is something deeply troubling with the account if it is not unitary – arises more naturally from a different view on the nature of moral theorizing: namely, that of the Direct View.

Some will object – strenuously, I think – that what I have just said borders on the unintelligible: 'What could possibly be meant by the moral point of view if you are to continue saying such things?' What lies behind this question is, of course, a conception about the very *nature of the moral point of view*: a conception nourished by the meta-ethical claim that any adequate moral judgement must express the impartiality of fairness, of judicial detachment, that attaches to many of our moral judgements. Hence such a critic is not raising a morally neutral claim, but a controversial one. And the one that is *at issue*, at that. For the question just is whether all moral judgements have a nature of the sort supposed, whether all moral dimensions to our lives possess a singularity. Hence this critic's question cannot be answered on the terms in which it is asked.[22]

Fair enough. But did not Hume insist that there is a 'steady and general' point of view from which moral matters are to be assessed, a point of view essential to sound moral judgement since it corrects various human propensities, like those of favoring our own interests, that otherwise lead us to erroneous moral judgements?[23] Does not that 'steady and general' point of view provide the unified account?

No. And the first point to be made in establishing Hume had no such intentions is that no presumption should be made that there is *one and only one* 'steady and general' point of view that is the object of Hume's concern. To assume this at the outset is to load the inquiry unfairly. It may be that speaking of *the* moral point of view or *the* steady and general point of view is the accepted *façon de parler*; but it is not an acceptable thought from which to begin. Moreover, Hume himself sometimes speaks of 'steady and general points of view.' (*T*, 581–582)

Hume's invocation of the 'steady and general points of view' is an essential ingredient in his model of the Judicious Critic. And as such, they apply (and are intended to apply) equally to whatever the Judicious Critic takes up for review: an essay, a painting, an oration, or a person's character. There is *nothing essentially moral* about them at all; anyone who gives even a cursory glance to *The Standard of Taste* cannot fail to see that, and any reasonable reading of the *Treatise* or *Inquiry* easily confirms the claim. So the 'steady and general' point of view does not characterize the artificial virtues in any essential way, nor does it provide any unitary account of the moral point of view. What role does it play in Hume's thought?

Hume recognized that a number of different kinds of judgements, which are united only by the fact that each has some basis in the 'senses,' are affected by factors such as distance from the object of perception, familiarity with the situation in which the object is seen, the frame of mind of the perceiver, and so forth. Such factors affect moral and aesthetic judgements just like they affect other judgements:

> Our situation, with regard both to persons and things, is in continual fluctuation ... Besides, every particular man has a peculiar position with regard to others; and 'tis impossible we cou'd ever converse together on any reasonable terms, were each to consider characters and persons, only as they appear from his peculiar point of view. In order, therefore, to prevent those continual *contradictions*, and arrive at a more *stable* judgement of things, we fix on some *steady* and *general* points of view; and always, in our thoughts, place ourselves in them, whatever may be our present situation. In like manner, external beauty is determin'd merely by pleasure; and 'tis evident, a beautiful countenance cannot give so much pleasure, when seen at the distance of twenty paces, as when it is brought nearer to us. We say not, however, that it appears to us less beautiful: Because we know what effect it will have in such a position, and by that reflexion we correct its momentary appearance.
>
> In general, all sentiments of blame or praise are variable, according to our situation of nearness or remoteness, with regard to the person blam'd or prais'd, and according to the present disposition of mind. But these variations we regard not in our general decisions, but still apply the terms expressive of our liking or dislike, in the same manner, as if we remain'd in one point of view. Experience soon teaches us this method of correcting our sentiments, or at least, of correcting our language ... Such corrections are common with regard to all the senses; and indeed 'twere impossible that we cou'd ever make use of language, or communicate our sentiments to one another, did we no correct the momentary appearance of things, and overlook our present situation. (*T*, 581–582)

The 'steady and general' point of view demands that our moral and aesthetic judgements – as well as a host of others that fit no such simple classifications – not be mere expressions of our actual sentiments. Instead the character of our judgements should be what anyone would feel upon appropriate contemplation of the object of judgement: judgements should be shareable, not the mere reflection of the 'peculiar' sentiments and situation of the judge. It follows that there is a clear sense in which judgements possessing that character are impersonal. They do not and must not have any essential references to oneself, as such; they are not merely an expression of *our* present sentiments, but those of a Judicious Critic. Such impersonality, though, is not identical to, nor does it imply, the impersonality of the sort required by the impersonal perspective of the artificial virtues. That standpoint is impersonal in the further sense that judgements made from it require that who a person is counts for naught: 'All the laws of nature which regulate property as well as all civil laws are general and regard alone some essential circumstances of the case, without taking in to consideration the characters, situations, and connections of the person concerned or any particular consequences which may result from the determination of these laws in any particular cases which offers.'[24]

Hume's concern in stating the case for a 'steady and general' point of view lies elsewhere. He wished to explain why the principles of taste are universal, and nearly the same in all men, and that these principles are the basis for all judgements of taste, *yet* many judgements and sentiments can be ignored because they are defective. The explanation is developed from the perspective that sets the inquiry: Hume considers the quality of any representative person's judgements from the perspective of a psychologist studying ontogeny. What explains the lack of delicacy in judgement? Coarseness? Lack of durability? Frivolousness? When you examine the various ways that the judgements of the inexperienced go awry, you can immediately see that a number of factors play a crucial role in *judicious* judgements of taste. Practical experience and acquaintance with the object of evaluation are necessary; and familiarity with other objects of this and comparable kinds is needed to insure that appropriate comparisons can be made, and necessary distinctions be drawn; personal prejudice, including cultural prejudice, must be tempered. Where good sense is wanting, so is the judiciousness necessary for sound judgements in matters of taste.[25] So Hume's move to the 'steady and general' point of view is a move from a perspective that is fleeting: the solipsistic viewpoint of our 'uncorrected' sentiments, sentiments characteristic of our earlier development. If they were to persist – which they cannot, due to sympathy[26] – continual 'contradictions' would arise and discourse would be impossible. Hence the need for some 'steady and general' point of view: a perspective that eliminates the deficiencies typical of our 'earliest' and 'uncorrected' sentiments, a perspective wherein judgements and sentiments of different parties generally concur.[27]

Hume's question – How do *we* come to see things as they are? – is a good one. And his answer recognizes, though probably not sufficiently, an important source – a set of sources, actually – of errors: self-deception, self-pity, self-aggrandizement, and other varieties of self projections that can prevent a person from seeing accurately. Practical thought does not begin after the facts are identified; it begins, if anywhere, with the identification of the facts. And this first task is not one which admits of practical neutrality.

For Hume, to take up a 'steady and general' point of view is to seek agreement, to be willing to try to correct one's natural propensities that lead to oversights, misinterpretation, and error. The impartiality of Hume's steady and general point of view is essentially that impartiality of mind we associate with nondogmatic inquiry. Question: Is there a single optimal viewpoint, from which all matters of taste (and hence moral conflicts and issues) are to be resolved? Or, are there several, perhaps many, 'steady and general' points of view? Must there be only one? Must there be some one common ground from which the correct basis for agreement is to be found among any disputants at any time? Do we *need* an assumption like that, say, of a positivist who maintains that what is *observable* is the common ground of adjudication among competing scientific theories?

The thought that there must be some *one* common ground of adjudication – something with or from which one could compel agreement – has had a long run in the history of moral thought. Figures as diverse as Plato, Hobbes, Bentham, Kant, and Sidgwick have helped to nurture and sustain it. But not Hume. He demands that we seek to eliminate the sources of variation in our practical judgements insofar as that is possible; our obligation is to seek agreement, to advance the best arguments, to use good sense, to inquire in an honest and open manner; but there is no guarantee that all diversity in judgement is unavoidable, that *all* differences can be reconciled, that rational and moral debate cannot be endless. Such guarantees are not part of our life any more than that the sun will rise tomorrow.

If we attend to the details of Hume's account of how we move from the partiality that characterizes our own 'peculiar' point of view to the 'steady and general' points of view from which we should make moral judgements – which I will refer to as a moral point of view – his official account reveals that a moral point of view is an *enlargement* of our 'peculiar' point of view;[28] it is an improvement that leads to less 'contradictions,' that secures agreement by mitigating the principal sources of variation. Take, for instance, our natural partiality for ourselves, our relatives, our countrymen. How is it circumscribed by moving to a moral point of view? Do we abstract from our particularity, refusing to consider any facts about ourselves or our relations to others that might promote partiality? Do we place ourselves behind a type of Kantian veil of ignorance?[29] No. Not at all. When we have a disregard for distant characters, due to our partiality for those close to us, we do not eliminate our closeness by abstracting from our particular relations; rather we remedy it by becoming *equally close* to what was previously distant:

> Our servant, if diligent and faithful, may excite stronger sentiments of love and kindness than *Marcus Brutus*, as represented in history; but we say not upon that account, that the former character is more laudable than the latter. We know that were we to approach equally near to that renown'd patriot, he wou'd command a much higher degree of affection and admiration. (*T*, 582)

What a splendid contrast. The Kantian move is to eliminate partiality, to eradicate it, by alienating oneself from any and every consideration that might contribute to partiality. (Kant, inspired by *Emile*, locked nature and freedom in opposition. We are viewed as oppressed by the bondage of nature that characterizes our existence after the fall. The essence of Kantian morality is the expression of reason in defiance of natural sentiments and inclinations;[30] it is the escape from their oppression, from the oppression of all things natural. Kant would have us alienate ourselves from the natural world of phenomena, of sensuous impulses and inclinations – where we have no control – to the world of noumena, where we are in complete control: a caustic reminder, if there ever was one, of the role of religion and metaphysics in moral thought.) Hume, instead, incorporates the partiality, forging a shared community of interest from it. If Kant's move is from the personal viewpoint of *me* to the thoroughly impersonal viewpoint of *whoever*, Hume's move is from *me* to *us*. For Hume my partiality is sufficiently mitigated if it is *shared* by others and others share mine. The partiality becomes ours: 'Being thus loosen'd from our first station, we cannot afterwards fix ourselves so commodiously by any means as a sympathy with those, who have any commerce with the person we consider.' (*T*, 583)[31] Clearly, this enlargement of one's 'peculiar' point of view does not result in the impersonal point of view presupposed by the artificial virtue of justice. Hence the 'steady and general' point of view that embodies this sympathetic sharing is not that of a morally unified account of our moral sentiments. It cannot even provide an account of the moral point of view presupposed by justice.

From where, then, does Hume procure the moral point of view presupposed by the artificial virtues? Aren't the artificial virtues 'invented' by molding and incorporating natural passions and sentiments, just as the 'steady and general' point of view is built upon and integrates features of our original, 'peculiar' point of view? Yes. Well, why isn't the moral point of view presupposed by the kind of virtues so created the one we just examined? Answer: the point of view so created is not a *moral* point of view at all. It is a point of view that characterizes nonsolipsistic perspectives and hence, any moral point of view must be consistent with it. But there is nothing essentially moral about it.

That being said, it remains that Hume does cheat. He sneaks a new conception of a moral point of view in the back door when he insists that justice must be thoroughly impersonal: *that* result is not due at all to the account of attaining a 'steady and general' point of view through the principle of sympathy, though Hume suggests, at times, that it is. Rather, it is related to the procurement of stable and enduring rules of property, without which a good life is impossible. Or so Hume thinks. There are, Hume avers, no exceptions to the rules of justice – exceptions of the sort that would be made, if personal considerations were allowed to affect and enter the rules of justice. Without this inflex-ibility, the system of rules would collapse. Why does Hume think this? Without a doubt, Hobbes' conceit has cast its shadow over Hume. The provenance of this queer thought, for the both of them, lies in the idea that the sword of justice must be wielded by an arbitrator with the status of a third party. The arbitrator must be thoroughly disinter-ested in the outcome of *any* dispute or conflict that comes before him, or else. Or else what? Or else he will wield his sword in his interest, others will perceive that justice has this interested character, and they will no longer have any reason to heed its dictates. Hence we must have such an impersonal arbitrator or no social order. No good life. Or, to modify the terms of discussion just a bit: there must be a moral point of view that is impersonal among individuals. Why? Because it plays the role of the disinterested arbitra-tor: it provides the fulcrum on which rules designed for *anyone*, for *whomever*, rest. There must be a common moral point of view to resolve all interpersonal conflicts, *or else*. Or else what? No social order. No good life. So there *must* be such a point of view, is the thought.

Hence one source of the idea of *the* moral point of view – of the idea that there is a thoroughly neutral perspective from which all interpersonal conflicts can be resolved – is the threat of what life would be like if there weren't such a neutral matrix.[32] But the threat is not real; it is only meta-physical. The surprise is that a hard-nosed, common-sensical person of Hume's caliber, someone who was such a keen observer of the human scene, was a victim of the subterfuge.

IX

Reflections on the Nature of the Beast

———————————◆———————————

Whether any particular person be endowed with good sense and
a delicate imagination, free from prejudice, may often be the
subject of dispute, and be liable to great discussion and enquiry
... Where these doubts occur, men can do no more than in
other disputable questions, which are submitted to the
understanding: They must produce the best arguments, that
their invention suggests to them. . . .

The Standard of Taste, 279

———————————

Morality, according to the Humean account, has two arti-
cles, the natural virtues and the artificial virtues, that cannot
be made entirely homogeneous. There is no harmonious,
unitary chronicle of morality, of our moral conscience, of
our moral sentiments; there is no single, optimal viewpoint
from which all moral questions must be addressed. Just as
there is no 'logically perfect' language in which philosophical questions are to be consigned, there is no 'morally perfect' point of view: no point of view from which all correc-
tions to our moral sentiments are made, nor any surety of
some final resting place in the process of correction. Moral
progress is not made nor measured in that way.

To be sure, Hume never articulates these conclusions as
forcefully as I have on his behalf; but they are implicit in
his thought; and, at times, are stated rather explicitly, as,
for instance, when he tells us that the partiality and unequal
affection we have for friends and relatives cannot be contracted so much that a person would 'give preference to a
stranger, or mere chance acquaintance' (*T*, 489), and yet,

that the rules of justice sometimes require us to follow a contrary course since 'it wou'd as often be an instance of humanity to decide contrary to the laws of justice as conformable to them.' (*T*, 579)[1]

Three concluding observations regarding the details and implications of Hume's thought, before proceeding to some more general reflections of that thought to the competition between the Direct and Indirect Views for our theoretical affections:

(1)   Hume's account of morality as a bicameral institution strikes me as both common-sensical and tremendously insightful. Even if we do not endorse the 'naturalness principle' that finances his natural virtues, nor his conception of rules of justice as inflexible and partial to complete impartiality, the division between the natural and artificial virtues is real. It carefully heeds two different sorts of interests, considerations, and demands of our moral life. The division is rooted in the conviction that a good person requires a good and relatively prosperous community to lead a good life: ethics and politics are inseparable sciences. But, as Hume notices, the relevant notion of a good community cannot be wholly captured by the artificial virtues, contra Hobbes and Mandeville. It must rely on some conception of the natural virtues. Hence Hume's idea that virtues are forged from the character of individuals as specified by the natural passions. By making this move of nesting virtue upon virtue to account for our sense of virtue, Hume rightly urges that any satisfactory chronicle of our refined moral sensibilities will display a familiar kind of circularity.[2] A person must have self-respect, which presupposes a conception of a good person living a good life. But that conception leads us to a catalogue of virtues specifiable only in terms of conceptions of a good community *and* a morally good person. And these latter two notions are not specifiable independently of each other. A good community must be understood as fostering justice and a good person must be understood as possessing the virtues, both natural and artificial. So any elaboration of the conceptions requires a bootstrapping circularity that will repeat the dialectic be-

tween the natural and artificial virtues: the natural virtues limit what the artificial virtues can be, in their scope and nature; the artificial are the product of the natural, but they are needed because the natural are too limited to govern moral life in more complex social orders; but the artificial do not supersede the natural virtues, and actually must foster them to procure a social order where human well-being will have its chance of satisfaction.

At the same time we should be aware that the metaphor of virtues being *built upon* virtues is just that: a useful metaphor for comprehending moral development and education. To understand the moral situation we often require metaphorical comparisons and idealized conceptions, such as the impartial demands of justice versus the demands of loved ones, the individualism of the contractual model of community whose moral relationships are defined by rights, as contrasted with the community whose relationships are defined by shared values, ends, and affections. These abstract models are legitimate devices for isolating some facet of our moral life for close scrutiny. But we should not be misled by our own tools. The legitimate purpose of these idealizations is to understand how a simplified world works. But the art of exemplary (systemic) moral thinking – and it is an art, a skill in the ancient Greek sense of a *technē* – is to appreciate when it is fruitful to bring the idealization to bear on the real world and when it is misleading or inappropriate, or, at times, even grotesque.

These abstract idealizations are not perfectly embodied in the practice of our lives; the idealizations blur, are partially realized, are rarely manifest. *Our* character, as revealed in our traditions, manners, rituals, habits, and attitudes – in the ways we converse with one another, work and play, worship and litigate, rear our children – is not so easily dissected. There will always remain residual patterns of behavior, rituals, and manners that express unspoken moral ideals: ideals that cannot be made fully express because their texture is rooted in the past and in our nature, but is open to the future. Just as a moral theorist cannot express every possible situation in which his principles are to apply, we cannot fully describe our character.

(2)   Hume's account of the moral sense is incomplete in the sense that no unified account is given or seems possible. It is certainly not regarded as necessary, as defective if absent. The natural virtues lack full accord with the artificial and the two seemingly cannot be rendered one without moral loss. From these facts we should not infer that the account cannot be made *coherent*: such an inference supposes a conception of theoretical unity (like that seen in the discussion of Sidgwick) that Hume does not share. And, in fact, according to the account developed, *challenges*.

We might express this difference between Hume and most members of the social contract tradition as a wager. The dominant theme found in the works of Locke and Hobbes and Kant is that justice is at its core a *contractual* notion that reveals our standing in relation to anonymous others. *And* that justice has a *primacy* in moral theory: it constrains and structures all other relationships and institutions that come under moral purview. These thoughts imply a theoretical wager on the part of the moral theorist who adopts them: namely, that the contractual model of relationships can be extended out from the core to encompass all that moral theory should address. As a theorist, you can make this wager or make book: the latter being a commitment to a nonunitary account of the Humean sort, the former a bet that the artificial virtues (or some appropriate theoretical analogue) will account for all the moral phenomena. Hume's genius is to see that this bet will be lost; that morality has no core of the sort supposed, but, rather, is better conceived on the model of a bicameral institution that is completed by describing the interaction and independent action of the separate houses; and that, in any case, the contractual model is not true to the facts since it cannot account for the *moral* nature and *moral* value of practices and relationships such as friendship and family.

How so? How is this contractual model inadequate if left unsupplemented? In two different ways. First, it relies on there being moral relationships on which it builds yet refuses to recognize. The artificial virtue of justice requires an extension of cooperation, fellow-feeling, and good will beyond the circle of one's family and friends, an extension that could not be made if these prior moral relationships were nonexistent, if they were relationships that also were to be contractually structured. Second, even if the contractual model got its footings without slippage – if justice-explicated-as-a-contractually-based-practice did not have to rely on *other* moral relationships to arrive on the scene – there are serious doubts that it can be extended to account for other moral relationships. The Kingdom of Ends helps us to understand one very important moral dimension of our lives: how we stand in relationship to others to whom we have no personal relationship; how and why free and equal adults have duties to one another and rights against each other.[3] But the very facts concerning impersonality and anonymity that structure the contractual nature of the relationships of people so conceived dictate that this model is not plausibly applied to other moral relationships such as, for example, those of intimate friends and companions, or parents and children. A model for a community of strangers is just that. And hence the traditional account of these relationships by liberal contractarian theorists as imperfect duties or relationships *permitted* by the principles of right. But, as we have seen, this path fails to explain the *moral* nature of such relationships by categorizing them with activities that are permitted because they have no moral standing (or only a secondary standing, as an 'extra' embellishment of social life that is not indispensable to it), and fails to account for the *double moral* value they can possess in virtue of their dual contribution to the good and the right.

Hume's account of our moral sense is also incomplete in a different sense: disregarding the issues of the unity of virtues, the moral sense is still not fully explainable. Hume's reason for thinking this lies in his understanding of the nature of explanation in the natural and practical sciences: namely, that any explanation, at bottom, requires an unexplained and unexplainable explainer which is itself grounded only in experience.

My inclination is to say that Hume has the right conclusion (that the moral sense is not fully explainable) but the wrong premises. Since he requires that morality be grounded in human nature, if we allow that any account of morality will need to refer to a distinction between the natural and artificial virtues, we can infer that such a grounding must be incomplete in this further sense. For, as we have seen, any such distinction has reflexive implications, all of which cannot be addressed by the distinction: no such distinction is fully *self*-accountable since it is ineluctably tied to the past and cannot anticipate all future experience. Hence any account of our moral sense in terms of it will be incomplete in this further sense. There is no terminus to moral progress and education. Or so our moral experience indicates.

(3) It is a most rare piece of moral theorizing that does not rely upon some view of human nature. And Hume is no *rara avis*. The puzzling discrepancy with Hume is that there seems to be not one, but two conceptions of human nature. Consider, first, the official version.

Hume was an established member of the Scottish Enlightenment, a member attempting to provide Natural Law – the natural jurisprudence of Grotius and Pufendorf taught in Scottish universities[4] by the highly esteemed Hutcheson – with a proper experimental basis. In particular, the 'religious hypothesis,' the asserted existence of God and his purpose for man, had to be exorcised from Natural Law to create a true science of man and politics.[5] He, like his oft quoted and beloved Cicero,[6] believed there to be a fundamental, unchanging human present throughout all social and cultural change: 'in all nations and ages ... human nature remains still the same, in its principles and operations.'[7] It is because justice is grounded so firmly in that nature that it is inalterable as well:

> Most of the inventions of men are subject to change. They depend upon humour and caprice. They have a vogue for a time, and then sink into oblivion. It may, perhaps, be apprehended, that if justice were allow'd to be a human invention, it must be plac'd on the same footing. But the cases are different. The interest, on which justice is founded, is the greatest imaginable, and extends to all times and places.

It cannot be possibly served by any other invention. It is obvious, and discovers itself on the very first formation of society. All these causes render the rules of justice stedfast and immutable; at least, as immutable as human nature.
(*T*, 620)

So we have the conception of human nature and justice as atemporal and ahistorical: *quod semper, quod ubique, quod ad omnibus*. These features are, no doubt, the primary source of the transcendental character of the moral point of view presupposed by the artificial virtue of Humean justice: for particularity of features and relationships cannot be recognized, as such, by invariant laws or viewpoints.[8]

When Hume approaches the natural virtues, he seems to lose his natural law bearings, if only momentarily.[9] The universal and invariable is spurned, almost with a vengeance, for affection for particular individuals, for concern for the good of specific people. Certainly a proper theoretical understanding of the interdependence of the natural and artificial virtues shows that our character, with its social and historical attributes, limits and distinguishes our moral thought; and hence any account that abstracts entirely from that character to elicidate the nature of our moral conceptions must be seriously mistaken.

Hume does not perceive this. Or at least not clearly by any means. He wavers at the edge, (almost?) apprehending the way things are and yet being torn away by his Enlightenment conception of the way things must be. He is close to an explicit (competing) view of human nature inseparable from its social *and* historical roots – a nature that can change and grow through time. How close? It's hard to say. But the *Standard of Taste* captures his honest refusal to lapse into his own certitudes:

But not withstanding all our endeavors to fix a standard of taste, and reconcile the discordant apprehensions of men, there still remain two sources of variation ... The one is the different humors of particular men; the other, the particular manners and opinions of our age and country. The general principles of taste are uniform in human nature ... But where

there is such diversity in the internal frame or external
situation as is entirely blameless on both sides, and leaves no
room to give one the preference above the other; in that case
a certain degree of diversity in judgement is unavoidable, and
we seek in vain for a standard, by which we can reconcile the
contrary sentiments.

A young man, whose passions are warm, will be more
sensibly touched with amorous and tender images, than a
man more advanced in years ... Vainly would we, in such
cases, endeavor to enter into sentiments of others, and divest
ourselves of those propensities, which are natural to us. We
choose our favorite author as we do our friend, from a
conformity of humor and disposition ...

One person is more pleased with the sublime; another with
the tender; a third with raillery. One has a strong sensibility
to blemishes, and is extremely studious of correctness;
Another has a more lively feeling of beauties, and pardons
twenty absurdities and defects for one elevated or pathetic
stroke ... Such preferences are indeed innocent and
unavoidable, and can never reasonably be the object of
dispute, because there is no standard, by which they can be
decided. (*ST*, 291–292)

It is a pity that Hume does not seem to comprehend fully
the tension; that his philosophical enthusiasm for natural
law and the Enlightenment ideals forces this aspect of his
thought to veer from 'the maxims of common sense,' to
become 'an experiment in a vacuum' not unlike those of
Diogenes and Pascal, of which he was most critical.[10]

X

Epilogue: Morality and Human Character

◆

From what has been said it is clear that all moral concepts have their seat and origin entirely a priori in reason ... they cannot be abstracted from empirical and hence merely contingent cognitions. In the purity of their origin lies their worthiness to serve us as supreme practical principles, and to the extent that anything empirical is added to them just this much is subtracted from their genuine influence and from the unqualified worth of actions ... since moral laws should hold for every rational being as such, the principles must be derived from the universal concept of a rational being generally. In this manner all morals, which need anthropology for their application to men, must be completely developed first as pure philosophy, i.e., metaphysics, independently of anthropology.

Foundations of the Metaphysics of Morals, Ak. 412–413

Which is correct: the Direct View? The Indirect View? Does the examination of Hume and Aristotle, Price, Reid, and Sidgwick reveal the truth? What is reflected from *this* inquiry into the history of ideas?

The Direct View, which has been in ascendancy as the research paradigm in moral philosophy (in Anglo-American thought) since the mid-nineteenth century, has, I think, reached a crucial juncture in its evolution. In the recent philosophical literature a groping dissatisfaction is evident both in the rising concern with the role of the virtues in morality – something which only recently has reemerged as a dominant topic of discussion after being the central focus of moral philosophy through the end of the 18th century – and the conception of rationality, practical reasoning and judgement associated with the Direct View. The relevance of the virtues to moral theory presents the most obvious challenge. For the virtues are tied to the character of persons and hence to complex personality structures. Therefore the human sciences of psychology, sociology, and anthropology have an obvious relevance to moral philosophy. But it is just this relevance that is denied by those identified as the chief *sources* of the Direct View as a research paradigm: Kant and Sidgwick.[1] Advocates of the Direct View tend to claim that psychology and related empirical disciplines have little or nothing to aid the moral philosopher in his understanding of morality, in his theory construction. Autonomy from them is proclaimed for moral theory. To be sure, the claim is not always made explicitly; often enough, it is concealed behind the facade of claims *about* the nature of morality or moral theorizing, advanced as manifest, banal truths. For instance, someone will ask, 'Well this piece on the virtues is interesting, but what is its relevance to moral theory?' Or commentators will puzzle over what Hume's ethical works are *about*, and will resolve their puzzle by noting that it is not work in moral theory per se, but in moral psychology; or that his theory, like that of the Greeks, is concerned with only a limited (and not the most important) range of moral appraisals, and even there primarily with their psychological nature.[2] But there is no sharp division between (moral) psychology and moral theory of the sort supposed. Furthermore if, as Hume asserts, morality must be grounded in human nature, the research program with a future will assimilate moral theory to psychology, anthropology, and sociology to a much greater extent. And must, like Hume, follow the course of historical and sociological realism. Why? Morality must make life better for those to whom it applies. It must be based in their nature and potentialities and an understanding of the nature of their social organizations: we must discover what practices and conventions improve, enlighten, and ennoble our lives, which cross desirable ends, 'stupefy the understanding and harden the heart, obscure the fancy and sour the temper.'[3] It is a fact about us that we learn about such things through experience, not through projects of pure inquiry: projects better suited to theological creatures who learn and know through ways not available to us.

In this section I want to gather some of the reflections that suggest the Direct View, as a research paradigm, has reached a turning point: that the power of its leading ideas no longer seem sufficiently attractive. The four topics that will be addressed are: (1) the question, broached by Hume's inquiry, whether there are ineliminable conflicts in morality; (2) the role of the 'naturalness principle' in moral theorizing; (3) further considerations about moral points of view; and (4) the role of character in practical thought. Although the issues will be treated separately, their divorce is manufactured: they are merely different facets of the same systematic pursuit.

(1) Why is a residuum of moral conflict thought to be a sign that our moral practices have not been fully rationalized? The rough idea is that the rational life is the life of creatures like ourselves, who need to employ reason because the demands of our complex nature are manifold and not always amicable. Hence it is inferred that practical intelligence must have as its goal the identification of priorities that, if followed, can purge the discord and thereby make people better off. Any rational conflict, therefore, is taken as a sign of incomplete rationalization.[4]

If we accept, for purposes of argument, this rough conception of the ends of rationality, we can locate some reasons for thinking it misguided. And consequently not be committed to the rejection of moral practices as rationally unjustified *solely* because they tolerate moral conflict.

First, any adequate moral theory must rely upon and be grounded in some conception of human nature[5] for a number of reasons, among which one of the most weighty, for present purposes, is that such a conception underwrites the confirmation of the relative success of its substantive principles: that is to say, it plays a decisive role in the appraisal of whether a moral practice makes creatures like *us* better off. Our moral practices are human ones. Our moral theories are about human justice, kindness, honesty, and friendship. Facts about us and our place in nature – that for instance, we are creatures tied to and constrained by our social and evolutionary history – bear on such theories. For that very reason, our theories do not apply to God or angels.

Second, if the conception of human nature is wanting, the moral theory it grounds will be similarly flawed. But, and this is the third point, any passable view of our nature will reveal the labyrinthine, knotty structure of our emotions, sentiments, needs, and feelings: what creatures like us are like and about. It follows that if any adequate view of our nature reveals clashes, *due to our nature*, that will ground moral conflicts, a strong presumption is created that all moral conflict is not eliminable in the manner suggested by the conception of practical rationality under examination. And the *facts* about us, as revealed through the lessons of history and the investigations of economists, biologists, psychologists, anthropologists, sociologists, and ethologists, support just such a view.[6]

To cite a few such facts. We are territorial creatures. We are possessive creatures, given to comparisons that can and do precipitate envy and jealousy. Flip what is the best in us over and you will discover that the very capacities and abilities that enable us to be noble, admirable creatures also fund what is dangerous and ignoble in our nature. Creatures like us who are capable of caring, of deep love and affection for others – capable even of attaching ourselves in this manner to places and ideas and causes – are *thereby* also capable of unswerving, irrational loyalty, of enthusiasm for false causes, of deception and jealousy and spite and intrigue, of irrational aggression. Again, our desire for respect, recognition, and status, our demand to be noticed, is a two-edged sword. As Hume showed, this complex aspect of our nature accounts for much of our pursuit of what is truly admirable and noble; yet it also feeds, at times, our appetite for malice, denigration, contempt, and futile and harmful gestures of self-importance. A hurt vanity is a most dangerous creature. So our *social* nature reveals both an admirable magnanimity and an ineliminable mean-spiritedness; what is best in us dictates that we do not live in harmony with everyone else.

And that there are limits to the implementation of an ideal, harmonious practice.

These considerations raise a very important issue that too often goes unaddressed in moral philosophy: the relationship between moral theories, that characteristically describe a complicated *ideal*, and our actual practices. If, for instance, we, like Hume and Aristotle, take the good person living the good life as the Alpha and Omega of serious moral inquiry, the issue can be confronted by assessing the manner and extent to which the ideal (at which we, as moral theorists, arrive) can be implemented: 'can,' as Hume was fond of saying, 'be reduced to practice.'

What we characteristically find is an abstract standard that must be applied, *imperfectly*, to some particular cases. For only as a fully abstract standard – say, as a representation of the unity of the central virtues – does it have any claim to being harmonious and unitary: only, that is, *before* it is applied in the various social and historical circumstances, circumstances to which it is supposed to apply to yield moral truths. The central virtues describe a *harmonious* set of possibilities, one that could be simultaneously realized in practice only in a Kingdom of Ends: something, *sans* euphemism, not practically possible. Such an ideal cannot be implemented in practice for a variety of reasons: bad luck, conditions spawned by things outside our control, e.g., the weather and natural disasters (such as earthquakes), and other historical contingencies. More important, though, are facts about us and the nature of evil. The harmony of the central virtues is realizable only when the perfect goodness of each person makes possible the coordination of the virtues in every detail of practice; the coordination is lost, and conflict results somewhere in the scheme whenever evil is present. So ineluctable facts about our nature make the harmonious union of virtues impossible. Wars, factions, intrigues, jealousies, envy, glory. How many are there who can step forward? Who have never been cruel? Vengeful? Wicked? Brutal? Dishonest? Who have never gloried in someone else's suffering?

To be sure, this clash between theory and practice can have other sources. Indeed, that is why it seems to me that

Hume's understanding of morality as a bicameral institution is important to us. If we take, so to speak, the left wing of the institution we get the Natural Law perspective expressed by Hume that tends to underwrite the moral (and legal) egalitarianism of liberalism: we are invited to see justice as a form of equality because that is what persons who are *totally* impartial – who are equal 'centers of interests' because their interests are identified in such a manner as to make them indistinguishable – would choose. But the extension of this perspective to all of practice produces discord between two or more different moral perspectives.

The commonplace and widespread conflict, in the practice of medicine, between considerations of a patient's autonomy and considerations of a patient's good seems to be of this sort. There is no a priori inconsistency between autonomy and beneficence; but, given the sort of world in which we live and the way we are, there is an inevitable tension and conflict between the two values, especially in certain avenues of life, as for example, in medicine.[7] It is a fact about us that we often need the same sort of comfort, support, and direction that we received as children when we find ourselves or loved ones to be seriously ill or injured. To tell physicians to respect autonomy *and* to seek their patient's health and well-being is to provide two perfectly correct dicta that all too often conflict in an irreconcilable way in practice. Only wishful thinking can harmonize the real conflict between the two values.

Or, to select a different topic, how can national boundaries be morally justified?[8] Or immigration laws? How can it be that arriving first, or being a descendant of someone who arrived first, provides one with a claim on some good (citizenship) if everyone's claims on goods are seen as equal from the spaceless and timeless perspective of morality? Again, if I am an employer, am I to choose who to hire on a morally neutral basis, a basis that prevents partiality to any particular features of persons, such as their nationality? Is it morally unjustified to refrain from hiring an alien because he is an alien? To refrain from hiring a stranger because he is a stranger? To refrain from hiring a friend because he is a friend? The contingencies – historical, social, and personal – create, at times, morally relevant considerations that cannot be countenanced from a timeless abstract perspective. To be sure, the moral conflicts such facts sire are not expressive of our nature, but are due to our circumstances. Thus there is always the modicum of hope that they can be totally eliminated. But such an assessment seems unwarranted and unduly optimistic. The same problems need not recur; but that hardly implies the absence of new ones. The conflicts created by changing circumstances are often real and painful, with no wholly equitable solution. For example, as the length of life changes – becoming longer both because we recognize (due to advances in medical technology) the beginning of a viable, normal human life occurring earlier in the term of pregnancy, and the normal life span of a human is extended through advances in medical and nutritional sciences – the social and economic order must change as well. Practices that were instituted for legitimate purposes become deficient and unfit in the new environment: e.g., social security, medical disability plans, rules governing retirement age. There are inevitable variances of interests, moral, economic, and social, in attempting to modify the existing practices. Groups with real and different interests clash and struggle; as conventions and practices are challenged, the moral reasons for acting they create and support are also challenged. For they are rooted in these contingent practices. Would that serendipity could be assumed for moral wisdom in practice, that we could have some providential assurance, some invisible hand.

(2) Hume, following Butler, asserted a naturalness principle, a principle that states some conduct is virtuous or worthy of moral approbation because it conforms to our nature. Implicit in any form of the naturalness principle is a reference to human nature: our nature is taken, depending on how the principle is worded, as a ground, the sole ground, or the standard for moral virtue and vice.

Obviously, the specification of our nature is a crucial matter to any theorist committed to some form of the naturalness principle. For, it would seem, only by first identifying our nature could we then proceed to identify what accords with it. Were that matters so simple.

They are not. Consider two of the more important gauges by which we identify what is natural to creatures like ourselves. First (as a rough, but passable approximation) we select features, traits or characteristics that are hard to eliminate, historically and culturally durable, generally possessed. Second, we identify something as natural if it is something of which we should approve its presence and which, if lost, makes a person worse off. Examples of the second sort would include a list of virtues: for example, courage, generosity, and civility. Clearly, items which are natural in this way are not of the sort mentioned in naturalness principles, unless such principles are utterly trivial. But items of the first sort, or at least some items of the first sort, seem just as inappropriate. Things that are natural in the first way form a very mixed bag: a sense of humor, for instance, seems just as natural in this sense as parental affection for children. As does self-deception, cruelty, hypocrisy, vengeance, and abuse of trust and power: each seems to be natural, to be expressive of our nature. But conduct that accords with *them* is hardly the beginning of virtue.[9]

The quick lesson to be learned is simply that there is *no morally neutral* way to identify what is natural in the appropriate sense. We identify things as being natural in the appropriate sense by (roughly) features such as historical and cultural durableness; but we recognize that not all things of this type are *important* to us. So further work needs to be done. But that further work requires moral conceptions to appraise the natural things, to select which are appropriate for use in a naturalness principle, a principle which *itself* yields moral conceptions of the type that underwrites the selection of things for use in a naturalness principle.

Hume, to be sure, thought otherwise. He took the neutral identification of the natural as a touchstone for moral theory building. Borrowing from the Stoics, he wished to replace their a priori identification of the features of human nature with a solid empirical foundation. It is ironical that Kant was inspired by the same Stoic fountainhead, and merely replaced what Hume had displaced, altering the object from human nature to rational nature. In Stoic thought the metaphysics of the identification of human nature (and hence our moral nature) was explicit: human nature must be understood as an aspect of the cosmos, all parts of which are governed by divine law, the law of reason, the *Logos*. What distinguishes man from other creatures and elevates him above them is his rational nature: he can become conscious of the *Logos*, the divine law of nature and reason, to which he necessarily conforms. And since the moral law is the law of reason, no man can become conscious of himself as a rational being without feeling committed to being a moral one.[10]

The classic Stoic argument illuminates not only the thoughts of Butler and Hume, but Kant as well. We can represent it as follows:

1 Every being pursues those things conformable to its nature, its essential constitution; and only such things have value for it.

2 Nothing can be conformable to the nature of a rational being unless it conforms to and proceeds from rational intelligence.[11]

3 Therefore, rational life constitutes virtue, because only virtue is good. [Virtuous conduct is conduct according to nature; vice is contrary to nature.]

Kant, inspired by these central ideas of Stoicism, restored the Stoic system in the modern dress of a Newtonian universe.[12] The physical laws that govern the cosmos provide an ironclad chain of causes from which no item in nature can escape; man is the center of the universe, capable of shaping society and history according to his conscious design; man can triumph over his animal nature, his physical side, through the creative activity of reason; only in this latter activity does man express his 'true' dignity and freedom; only when man acts from the Moral Law, the expression of Reason, only when his conduct is not determined by sensuous desires or contingent aims, does he realize his 'true' self; only the man of moral worth can, therefore, overcome necessity of the natural order through his transcendental freedom, his participation in the timeless objects of reason.

(3) If we follow Hume's thought we forsake the pursuit of *the* moral point of view, settling for moral points of view. Exactly what do we forsake, why, and at what cost?

The moral point of view sought by Kant, the moral point of view presupposed by Hume's artificial virtues, what Burke called 'the eternal frame of the Universe,' each represents a quest for a representation *sub specie aeternitatis*, from the complete and absolute impersonality of the Universe. Why is such a search initiated? A chief rationale is the *fear* about what morality would be like if such a unique point of view does not exist. The fear can be represented by reference to what I have termed Hobbes' 'or else' argument. Unless there is a *wholly disinterested, absolutely neutral* point of view from which to resolve moral conflicts, they will be resolved, if at all, from some interested point of view; but all parties to conflicts will not have reasons to need *such* resolutions, and since such resolutions are moral solutions to practical problems, it follows that people do not have reasons to be moral, to see the principles of morality as providing reasons for them to act. Morality would lose its authority and legitimacy.[13]

What will quell this fear? Some final, absolute resting place, either one that settles all things for all times, or one that can be called upon at any time to settle anything: an ultimate court of appeals, if you will.[14]

The search for a wholly neutral, disinterested point of view – *the* moral point of view – seems destined to futility because all viewpoints reflect the interests that caused them to arise. There are no classifications, selections, or, if you prefer, descriptions, that are totally disinterested: such things would exist only if classifying and describing were the characteristic activities of cameras, instead of humans. If we wish to use this locution of 'points of view,' we need to acknowledge that there is no single optimal point of view. There are many points of view, and each provides an interpretation of data, of considerations gained from that perspective, of classifications that reflect and direct our thought. Hume demanded that the data, so interpreted, be made consistent with what we know could be obtained from other viewpoints. And such a model of converging viewpoints makes good sense if we are thinking about visual perception (though even here the assumption of a unique point of convergence is unwarranted). When I observe shadows cast across the lawn by the setting sun, I can correct my perceptual judgement by taking into account features peculiar to my perspective, my angle of vision, my near-sightedness, my inattentiveness due to the swarming flies. I can recognize and discount these various factors. But, although moral judgement often requires discounting irrelevant factors as well, the spatial metaphor of points of view, suggesting that moral judgements are like matters of vision, is inapt. The different viewpoints, in the case of morality, are not limited to different 'spatial' perspectives characterizable by *locating* the perceiver and describing the conditions of perception; differences such as age, practical experience, sex, historical situation, and temperament play roles in the moral case that preclude any useful conception of a *normal* observer, modeled after a normal perceiver. For the specification of a normal observer merely raises again the question whether that provision can be made in a morally neutral manner, from a wholly disinterested point of view. It cannot. The search for the fabled exclusive viewpoint is, in reality, a search for the *absence* of any point of view: to wit, the timeless, non-spatial perspective of no one.

The absence of such an exclusive moral point of view need not undermine the legitimacy of morality; there is no need to believe that to elude the partial standpoint of a particular observer or set of observers you need to assume a perspective which no observer can assume. The argument for this claim rests on a false dichotomy. It is thought that to obtain a *pure* confrontation with the moral situation – pure because untainted by any particular person's interests that would infect the point of view and uncontaminated by any local or parochial interests – you need a transhistorical perspective that must be relevant to all moral inquiry, past, present, and future. But this thought is grounded in the notion that you can represent things without any reference to the interests of people – a representation that is thoroughly impartial – or you can have a partial representation of things by permitting interests to be reflected in your representation. Such a division, if true, would license the (bad) inference from 'one cannot represent things without any reference to the interests of persons' to 'there are no impartial representations of things.' So, one who accepts the (false) dichotomy *and* the fact that all points of view reflect the interests that brought them into existence, seems committed to moral impartiality being a sham, a mere smokescreen.

Why is this line of thought defective? Why is the dichotomy that fathers it untrue? Simply because the relevant sense of *impartial* is nothing more than *conduct that does not favor the interests of any parties unfairly*; conduct is unbiased and impartial even if it is not the result of a disinterested viewpoint, even if it is selfishly motivated. The degree to which conduct is impartial is not a function of the beliefs and desires of the agent; whether a situation is described impartially is not a function of whether the descriptions fail to refer to interests that could cause a partial presentation.

Finally, what do we lose if we forsake the quest for a transcendental perspective outside all moralities and all moral theories, a perspective from which we are supposed to be better suited to estimate the adequacy of these social products? A quick answer: the possibility of any account that makes the rejection of moral skepticism, egoism or relativism inescapable. An account that would reduce these doctrines to a par with those of the Flat Earth Society.

Surely this is no loss at all. For these doctrines, in their more sophisticated forms, are not *utterly* unreasonable. Yet that is what must be shown to compel their rejection: something like the fact that they are internally inconsistent. The fact of the matter is that these doctrines, if unappealing, are so because they are not the most reasonable views; but they are hardly on the borders of unreason.

(4) The Direct View, in its secular form, got its footings at the time of and, I believe, through the development of the

social contract as a philosophical vehicle to illustrate the
nature of morality and moral agency. This was and is a
quite natural evolution of the themes, both metaphysical
and moral, that have been, and are, the chief preoccupations
of advocates of the Direct View. In this section I will
attempt to portray, albeit only too briefly, this last aspect of
the terrain.

It was the central demand of the *Aufklärung*, as Kant saw
it, *not to accept anything contingent as authoritative*: that
institutions or practices exist, that they are supposedly
rooted in the nature of things, lends them no legitimacy.
All authority must be shown to be justified before the sacred
tribunal of reason, which alone can determine the true
worth of any thing.

> Is it not of the utmost necessity to construct a pure moral
> philosophy which is completely freed from everything which
> may be only empirical and thus belong to anthropology? That
> there must be such a philosophy is self-evident from the
> common idea of duty and moral laws. Everyone must admit
> that a law, if it is to hold morally, i.e., as a ground of
> obligation, must imply absolute necessity; he must admit that
> the command, 'Thou shalt not lie,' does not apply to men
> only, as if other rational beings had no need to observe it.
> The same is true for all other moral laws properly so called.
> He must concede that the ground of obligation here must not
> be sought in the nature of man or in the circumstances in
> which he is placed, but sought *a priori* solely in the concepts
> of pure reason, and that every other precept which rests on
> principles of mere experience, even a precept which is in
> certain respects universal, so far as it leans in the least on
> empirical grounds (perhaps only in regard to the motive
> involved), may be called a practical rule but never a moral
> law.[15]

All legitimate practices and structures, therefore, must be
shown to be an effect of the exercise of rational wills, *acting
as such*. Hence to carry out the project of justification one
needs to segregate that which is constitutive of our rational
nature, as such, from that which holds merely contingently
for rational creatures like ourselves. So the first thing to

118

notice is that the project supposes that we can discover the essence of rationality, its timeless nature, and contrast it with claims about rationality that may be false. But much of the recent work in philosophy of science and metaphysics has discredited any distinction of this sort.[16]

How important is a distinction of this type to the whole project? It's no small matter. For it plays a central role in revealing the justificatory force of principles identified by the social contract.

Consider: the social contract represents a hypothetical situation of choice. The contract specifies the principles to which the parties agree in that imagined situation. What can such a contract secure for a moral theorist? Well, the problem is one of justification: of revealing, say, that our present practices are not merely arbitrary, but, rather, are legitimate, because they would be chosen by rational agents in the situation of choice specified by the model of the social contract. But if we cannot detach what is essential to rationality from what is contingently true of it, the chief methodological purpose for the social contract is undercut. For the self-grounding that arrests the search for a justification, that halts the quest for political and moral legitimacy, is reputed to work just *because the choices are supposed to reflect only reason, as such.* That self-grounding is viewed as a creation of reason itself: something that is *both a reason and a cause.* And this magic works only if we locate reason, as such: that is, the formal or categorical structure of reason.

The Hobbesian idea that the moral and political order can be justified by the appeal to such a contract, while one simultaneously sheds some light on the *generation* of that same order, is rooted in the idea of rationality as both a reason and a cause. There is also an implicit reference to individuals as the causal agents who bring about the moral and political order through their rational wills: the moral (and political) order is seen as a product of individuals, as the product of the agreement revealed in the social contract. This is merely an extension of the thought that *ultimate* reasons must be causes, viewed against the backdrop of *man's elevation to the center of the universe* in virtue of his rationality. But any such reconstruction thereby becomes tied to the untenable doctrines of philosophical individualism. Moreover, it seems inevitably wed to a conception of our powers – over our institutions and nature – that attributes too much to us. (Perhaps it likens reason's capacity to transform the world, to create *de novo* the moral universe through an act of will, too much to God?)

Social practices and institutions, including the moral order, are not the intended product of deliberate action; the moral order cannot be explained or illuminated through a representation of it as the end result of a contract among rational agents considered as such. Such attempts characteristically fail, as Hume so perceptively noted, because they implicitly presuppose the existence of *exactly* that which they try to explain. But it is important to note that whether this criticism applies to the Kantian attempt, it suffers from a different, though related, defect. On the Kantian model, rational agents, *as such*, are identified as those who are placed behind the veil of ignorance. Recall, the veil functions, or is supposed to function, to prevent what is merely contingent from affecting the individual's choices.[17] Persons behind it are ignorant of facts about themselves and their circumstances, their social institutions and practices (as theirs), and, in general, any fact that can affect their choice by making it partial, by making it not represent the choice of a rational agent, as such.

Kant's various descriptions of a will motivated solely by respect for the *form* of a maxim lucidly establish that rational agents, as such, cannot be affected by any of their contingent psychological states; the veil must screen not just facts about their interests, but their emotions, cares, motives, and personal attitudes. It must, in short, purge their *character*, save what psychological states they can be said to have solely in virtue of being rational.[18]

What remains behind such a veil? The essence of a rational will: a will realizing its own nature; a will that cannot be understood as a part of the natural order of things; a will that stands above the natural order, expressing itself by bringing into existence in the natural order a moral universe not found there.

In effect, then, we find a standard of rationality represented by one chooser. Why one? Because any arbitrary rational agent, as such, is the chooser; and any such agent is not distinguishable from any other, possessing only those properties that are common to all. Here we have a unitary depiction of rationality: the transcendental point of view of a rational person, as such.

Or do we? The standards of rationality, like all benchmarks of evaluation, have some reference, implicit or explicit, to the shared evaluative conceptions of other members of the social order. The idea of rationality as free floating and hence disinterested, because it is untied to any interests, the idea of rationality as something specified *and realized completely independently of institutions, social practices, and culture* – as wholly self-contained and self-sufficient – is a contrivance of the philosophical mind. Practical rationality simply cannot be segregated from our character in the required manner, nor can it become solitary.

Our evaluative conceptions do not, and cannot, develop in a social vacuum, nor exist in one. Consider, for the moment, our norms and standards of right-living, which are sufficiently like the canons of practical rationality to provide a useful point of comparison.

Our evaluative conceptions about the nature and ideals of right-living are drawn from vast networks of social activities that have transpired over enormous reaches of time: models of conduct and character have been established, assayed, rejected, confirmed, revised, redrawn, shown unfit. The process continues. We *identify* with such models, taking them to be what we should be like, what we want to *be*. Our admiration and esteem for those whose character and conduct we approve and respect causes us to desire to become like them, to become the objects of such approval and respect. Such identifications are integral to the continuing process, for they connect the standards to the various patterns of behavior characteristic of the process, making us the sort of rational creatures that we are. We can ignore these systematic internal connections between a person's motivational structure, his sentiments, and the evaluative conceptions only with great peril. *Identifications* are morally and psychologically transforming, a part of *our* rationality;

without them we could not understand the moral and rational behavior of creatures like us.

Without reference to identifications, or some comparable explanatory element, we could not understand the rational behavior of creatures like ourselves: why we care about the standards of rationality, apply them to others' behavior, feel ashamed when we bend them, engage in self-reproach. Identification allows us to understand the connection between the statement of the norm and why the norm affects the person's behavior, attitudes, motivation, and feelings: in a word, how and to what extent the norm expresses and reflects his character.

But, given the description of the veil of ignorance, no identifications are possible behind it. There are no identifications in a social vacuum; no identifications can be realized independently of social practices and institutions. And identifications have no place in a one person social order.

Our character cannot be separated from the nature and standards of practical thought in the way some social contract theorists suggest. There may be some respects in which we are like God, but this is not one. This point should, I think, be generalized. Inquiry of any sort – scientific or moral, historical or philosophical or literary – relies upon moral virtues such as honesty, charity, and fair-mindedness. The pursuit of truth relies upon the character of its inquirers; it certainly is not separable from their character.

Notes

---◆---

I What is Morality all About?

1 Alan Donagan, *The Theory of Morality* (Chicago: University of Chicago Press, 1977), 29.
2 *Ibid.*, 54.
3 *Ibid.*, 55.
4 Here I do not mean to imply that the Direct View cannot apply as well to large slices of life, as, for example, when one asks oneself what he should be doing in the next several years. General rules of direction and revisable strategies certainly can play a role in deliberative contexts.
5 To be sure, Kant's theory is radically different from Martineau's, and seems more sympathetic, in one sense, to the posture of theorists who support the Direct View. For *if* you read Kant as attempting to provide a decision procedure for appraising the moral quality of any act, he certainly appears to have one foot, perhaps both feet, in the Direct camp. Nevertheless, it is clear that Kant believed that we arrive at adequate procedures for the appraisal of acts by first providing a theory about the *nature* of moral agency, and proceed *from it* to substantive rules and principles that govern conduct. And that first task is a necessary first task. Kant attempts to derive the Categorical Imperative, the principle that grounds all moral principles of conduct, from the notion of a type of agency: that exemplified by the person of good will.

II Sidgwick: The Direct View

1 My understanding and treatment of Sidgwick is greatly indebted to J. B. Schneewind's definitive study in his *Sidgwick's Ethics and Victorian Moral Philosophy* (London: Oxford University Press, 1977).
2 Henry Sidgwick, *The Methods of Ethics* (Chicago: University of Chicago Press, 1962 reprint of seventh edn), 26, 32, 37.
3 Henry Sidgwick, *The Methods of Ethics*, first edn, my emphasis, 25–26.
4 See, e.g., Bernard Williams, 'Ethical Consistency,' in *Problems of the Self* (New York: Cambridge University Press, 1977), 175f.; Herbert Morris, 'Persons and Punishment,' *The Monist*, 52 (1968), 498–499;

123

Ruth Barcan Marcus, 'Moral Dilemmas and Consistency,' *Journal of Philosophy*, 78 (1980), 121–136.

5 *Ibid.*, 175f.

6 For a rationalist resolution that opts for the last candidate, see Alan Donagan's most interesting piece, 'Consistency in Rationalist Moral Systems,' *Journal of Philosophy*, 81 (1984), 291–309. I discuss several of Donagan's arguments below.

7 We may be fortunate to live in a world where it *just so happens* that things will work out satisfactorily often enough if you employ the agglomeration principle in such judgements, but that hardly establishes *its* reliability as a principle of inference.

8 For further details see the discussion in Chapter X.

9 Alan Donagan, 'Consistency in Rationalist Moral Systems,' *Journal of Philosophy*, 81 (1984), 291–309.

10 *Ibid.*, 306.

11 If he insists that design coordination in these cases can be gained only dialectically, as they occur and need be addressed, what can ground his confidence that all conflicts will disappear?

12 My suspicion is that this emphasis on the rule of law is a somewhat misguided rationalist extension of a principle that is quite appropriate and needed where it was first put to work. We want our judiciary to have very limited discretion; we do not want personal judgements, as such, to function as law. A judicial system which permits much unbridled and unprincipled judicial discretion – a system found all too often in, for example, the history of Europe – is too unreliable and inequitable. Hence there was a strong rationale for demanding public procedures that severely curtailed the power of the judiciary. But it seems to me that rationalists have tended to use this perfectly apt political principle as an epistemological model for the representation of moral knowledge: all such knowledge must be replicable through a codification of laws and procedures which are more adequate, *ceteris paribus*, to the extent that good judgement is eliminated from the scene and the correct results can be generated mechanically. The codification represents the rationalist's means of surmounting the traditional understanding of the connection between practical wisdom and experience: any gaps thought to be created by inexperience are closed by the system of laws and procedures.

III Moral Virtues and the Direct View

1 See, e.g., William Frankena, *Ethics*, 2nd edn (Englewood Cliffs, N.J.: Prentice-Hall, 1973), 62–70, and 'Pritchard and the Ethics of Virtue,' *The Monist*, 54 (1970), 1–17; G. E. M. Anscombe, 'Modern Moral Philosophy,' *Philosophy*, 33 (1958), 1–19; Myles Burnyeat, 'Virtues in Action,' in *The Philosophy of Socrates*, ed. G. Vlastos (Garden City, N.Y.: Doubleday, 1971), 209–234; Stephen Hudson, 'Taking Virtues Seriously,' *Australasian Journal of Philosophy*, 59 (1981), 189–

202; Alasdair MacIntyre, *After Virtue* (Notre Dame, Ind.: University of Notre Dame Press, 1981).

2 The first criticism of this tendency was made by J. O. Urmson in his 'Saints and Heroes,' in *Essays in Moral Philosophy*, ed. A. I. Melden (Seattle: University of Washington Press, 1958), 198–216.

3 See: Joel Feinberg, 'Supererogation and Rules,' *International Journal of Ethics*, 71 (1961), 276–288; Roderick Chisholm, 'Supererogation and Offence: A Conceptual Scheme for Ethics,' *Ratio*, 5 (1963), 1–14.

4 Feinberg, *ibid.*, 1–4; Richard Brandt, 'The Concepts of Obligation and Duty,' *Mind*, 73 (1964); C. H. Whiteley, 'On Duties,' *Proceedings of the Aristotelian Society*, 53 (1952–53); H. L. A. Hart, 'Are There Any Natural Rights?,' *Philosophical Review*, 64 (1955), 175–191.

5 W. D. Ross, *Foundations of Ethics* (London: Oxford University Press, 1939), 146.

6 W. D. Ross, *The Right and the Good* (London: Oxford University Press, 1930), 16–47.

7 For example, in *The Metaphysical Elements of Justice*, he writes:

> The categorical imperative, inasmuch as it asserts an obligation with regard to certain actions, is a morally practical law. But, because obligation includes, not only practical necessity (of the sort that a law in general asserts), but also constraint, the imperative mentioned is a law of either command or of prohibition, according to whether the performance or the nonperformance is represented as a duty. An action that is neither commanded nor prohibited is merely allowed, because with respect to it there is no law that limits freedom (competence) and, therefore, also no duty. Such an action is called morally indifferent (*indifferens, adiaphoron, res merae facultatis*). . . .
>
> A conflict of duties (*collisio officiorum s. obligationum*) would be a relationship between duties by virtue of which one would (wholly or partially) cancel the other. Because, however, duty and obligation are in general concepts that express the objective practical necessity of certain actions and because two mutually opposing rules cannot be necessary at the same time, then, if it is a duty to act according to one of them, it is not only not a duty but contrary to duty to act according to the other. It follows, therefore, that a conflict of duties and obligations is inconceivable (*obligationes non colliduntur*). [223–224]

8 John Stuart Mill, *Utilitarianism* (Indianapolis: Bobbs-Merrill, 1971), 47–48. Mill proceeds to warn that writers who fail to make this distinction will tend 'to merge all morality into justice.'

For two helpful discussions in the secondary literature, see: David Lyons, 'Human Rights and the General Welfare,' *Philosophy and Public Affairs*, 6 (1977), 113–129; Jonathan Harrison, 'The Expedient, the Right, and the Just in Mill's *Utilitarianism*,' *Canadian Journal of Philosophy, Supp. Vol.*, 1 (1974), 93–107.

9 For an excellent summary of the various ways in which Kant attempts

to draw the distinction between perfect and imperfect duties, and the numerous resulting problems, see: Paul Eisenberg, 'From the Forbidden to the Supererogatory: The Basic Ethical Categories in Kant's *Tugendlehre*,' *American Philosophical Quarterly*, 3 (1966), 255–269; Thomas E. Hill, Jr., 'Kant on Imperfect Duty and Supererogation,' *Kant-Studien*, 62 (1971), 55–76.

10 Samuel Pufendorf, *De Jure Naturae Et Gentium Libri Octo*, tr. Oldfather and Oldfather (Oxford: Clarendon Press, 1934 reprint of 1688 edn), 118. Cf. 302–305, 314–315, 627–629.

11 This case is discussed by Michael Stocker in his 'The Schizophrenia of Modern Ethical Theories,' *Journal of Philosophy*, 63 (1976), 453–466. See also Lawrence Blum, *Friendship, Altruism and Morality* (London: Routledge & Kegan Paul, 1980), and Bernard Williams, 'Persons, Character and Morality,' in *Moral Luck* (Cambridge: Cambridge University Press, 1981), 1–19.

12 Marcia Baron, in a most interesting defense of Kant from his modern foes, recognizes this point but attempts to deflect it by insisting that the Kantian notion of duty encompasses acts that one morally ought to do, and such acts can be of one of two sorts: either morally required or morally recommended. Hence Baron regards these acts of friendship as morally recommended, though not morally required: see her 'The Alleged Repugnance of Acting From Duty,' *Journal of Philosophy*, 81 (1984), 199–201.

The idea that duty is a concept specified by considerations that an act is morally required *and/or* that it is morally *recommended* puzzles me. If duty is construed in the Kantian fashion of what one ought to do being the (philosophical) definition of 'duty,' I have no complaints but that it obscures the nature of the moral phenomena it encompasses. (Unless one equivocates: see notes 14 and 15 below.) But Kant made all acts Baron recognizes as morally recommended but not required into imperfect duties. And the reason for this lies, in part, in the fact that he held that the fact that an act is morally required entails that it would be wrong to fail to do it, and, that an act is not required entails that it is not wrong to fail to do it. But Baron cannot, I think, concur. For if there are cases where morality recommends something and does not require it (e.g., the case at hand), she tells us that one ought to do it and to fail to do it would be wrong. But now, if Kant's conception is brought to bear on the case at hand, the act is not morally required and hence is not wrong to fail to do, but is morally recommended and hence is wrong to fail to do.

13 It bears saying that I have not yet established that friendship or moral virtues such as generosity or civility do, in fact, possess a double moral value in the way I am describing. Here my goal is merely to depict the nature of such value; the discussion of Aristotle and Hume will serve as the vehicle to show that many virtues possess such a double moral value.

14 William Frankena, *Ethics*, 13.

15 And, of course, it does. But we must remember that it is a *philosophical* sense: one invented by philosophers.

126

16 That *some* acts of virtue are not obligatory in this sense either does not affect the argument. An act, say of friendship or generosity, that is a morally good act, but not one that is impermissible not to perform, is an example of another type of moral value that should also be addressed by a moral theorist. But the point asserted here is that a philosophical definition of 'obligatory' to mean 'impermissible not to ...' does not determine or in any way settle whether acts that fall under this definition are duties or obligations (in a non-technical sense) or virtues. What acts fall under the definition and what their character is cannot be settled by linguistic imperialism.

17 William Frankena, *Ethics*, 65, emphasis mine.

18 *Ibid.*, 66–67.

19 Such sharp distinctions are favored by those who continue, *in practice*, to favor analyses in terms of necessary and sufficient conditions as philosophically informative. These analyses fail miserably when applied to multi-dimensional terms and concepts. And so it is with acts and agents. Among the reasons why a sharp distinction between acts and agents is untenable is that our classifications of actions into types *serves many different purposes*; and since the distinction is drawn in relation to the purposes, *there is no fixed, once and for all way to draw it*. We group acts together as a type for a variety of reasons: e.g., their effects, their characteristic purpose, their characteristic intent. And it makes no sense to distinguish sharply between features of an act and features of an agent when the features that characterize the act just are features of some agent. Nor does it make any sense to insist that one type of classification of acts must serve as a model for all others: e.g., that distinctions drawn in civil law will be the same as in criminal law, that in law the same as that in etiquette.

20 Lawrence Blum, *Friendship, Altruism and Morality* (London: Routledge & Kegan Paul, 1980), 141f.

21 I give you some of the surplus tomatoes from my bountiful crop. (I take them to your house and leave them on the back porch.) Why is my behavior correctly described as an act of giving you the tomatoes? There are many acts I can perform, each of which requires that I place the tomatoes on your porch, but none of which is an act of giving you the tomatoes. (I could repay you for those I borrowed earlier. I could add some more to your account. I could set them there until I could retrieve them later.) Is there any exhaustive specification of overt behavior that insures my act is one of giving you the tomatoes?

This example is a slightly amended version of one proposed by G. E. M. Anscombe in her 'On Brute Facts,' *Analysis*, 18 (1958), 69–72. See also Iris Murdoch's discussion in her *The Sovereignty of Good* (New York: Schocken, 1971), 17–18.

22 See, e.g., Myles Burnyeat, 'Virtues in Action,' in *The Philosophy of Socrates*, ed. G. Vlastos (Garden City, N.Y.: Doubleday, 1971), 209–234; G. H. von Wright, *The Varieties of Goodness* (London: Routledge & Kegan Paul, 1963), 144–148; Richard Brandt, 'Traits of Character: A Conceptual Analysis,' *American Philosophical Quarterly*, 7 (1970),

23–37; Terry Penner, 'The Unity of Virtue,' *Philosophical Review*, 82 (1973), 44–48.

23 James Martineau, *Types of Ethical Theory*, 2 vols., 1885. For a penetrating commentary, see Schneewind's *Sidgwick's Ethics and Victorian Moral Philosophy*.

24 See, e.g., Richard Brandt and Jaegwon Kim, 'Wants as Explanations of Actions,' *Journal of Philosophy*, 60 (1963), 425–435; Carl Hempel, 'Logical Positivism and the Social Sciences,' in *The Legacy of Logical Positivism*, ed. P. Achinstein and S. Barker (Baltimore: Johns Hopkins Press, 1969), 170–173; Paul Churchland, 'The Logical Character of Action Explanations,' *Philosophical Review*, 79 (1970), 214–236; Stephen Darwall, 'Practical Skepticism and the Reasons for Action,' *Canadian Journal of Philosophy*, 8 (1978), 251–254.

IV Aristotle: The Indirect View

1 The expression 'human excellence' is a more satisfactory rendering of Aristotle's *ethike arete* than 'virtue.'

2 *Nicomachean Ethics*, 1105b5–8.

3 The failure to take in relevant features of the situation is often due to one's moral character; what you are sensitive to, what you notice, neglect, apprehend, or slight is a function of character. It is an interesting fact that such failures are moral failures: they are held to be wrong in the same manner that acts are wrong. This suggests that the view that what morality is all about is acts and their evaluations is too narrow.

4 My understanding of Aristotle is much indebted to James Wallace's 'Excellences and Merit,' *Philosophical Review*, 83 (1974), 182–199.

5 *Nicomachean Ethics*, 1105a29–35.

6 For purposes and illustration and contrast I have spoken of acts being generous, claiming that such acts are merely typical of generosity. This is a point not reflected in our language. If I say 'That was a generous thing to do,' that will normally imply either that the act was an expression of generosity or at least characteristically motivated for generosity. We hardly ever *speak* of an act of generosity if it was merely what a generous person would have done. (The distinction is there, but not marked by our ordinary expressions.) In this way the language of some virtues (for example, generosity) differs from others (for example, honesty). For we do regularly say such things as 'He only did what was honest,' without implying anything about his reasons or motives.

7 The notion of 'dictates or precepts of courage' should not be taken to imply that a person must act while keeping in mind some principle or precept referring specifically to courage. Courage is like kindness: a kind person need not possess an articulate conception of kindness which enters into his thought and reasoning. It is enough if, among other things, his acts of kindness are performed under some description such as 'I must do this,' or 'This is the thing to do.'

Nor should the notion of such 'dictates,' or 'principles,' or 'precepts' be thought to smuggle in the Direct View through the back door. It would only if the content of the principles could be specified without reference to the virtues themselves. And that is not intended. The content of the principles makes essential reference to an ideal of a person, which in turn is used to identify acts that express that ideal, and without which, those acts could not be identified.

8 The sense of *identification* employed here is technical: roughly, I employ the notion to refer to the psychological processes whereby models of persons or character we admire, esteem, approve, or respect cause us to desire to become like them, to be persons like them. See my discussion of Hume in Chapter VI.

9 'Vice (*kakia*) is unconscious of itself, weakness of will is not ... Evidently, then, weakness of will is not a vice (though perhaps it is so in a qualified sense); for weakness of will is contrary to choice while vice is in accordance with choice.' *Nicomachean Ethics*, 1151a1–7.

10 The Pliable Dodger's resolve to act in accordance with the principles of honesty is weak. To be honest one must have the strength of will to hold one's resolve when and if one is inclined to act otherwise. So the Pliable Dodger exhibits one sort of deficiency in honesty. One can imagine a close relative – the Backsliding Dodger – whose problem also is, in some sense, a deficiency in commitment to the principles of honesty. What characterizes him is that often enough, when honesty is called for, he backslides and decides that, after all, in this situation he may forgo honesty. Here is another sort of deficiency.

It goes without saying that if any of the Dodgers wed someone from the family of Self-Deception, the complexities of their psyches grow exponentially.

V Further Reflections on Acts and Agents

1 Here I am indebted to A. N. Prior's 'The Virtue of the Act and the Virtue of the Agent,' *Philosophy*, 26 (1951), 121–130, which discusses Price's work and its relation to other historical figures. All references to Price's *Review* (London: Oxford University Press, 1948 reprint of 3rd edn, 1787, ed. D. D. Raphael) will be identified in the text by '*R*' followed by the page number: e.g., [*R*, 198].

2 Thomas Reid, *Essays on the Active Powers of the Human Mind* (Cambridge, Mass.: M.I.T. Press, 1969 reprint), 394. Reid continues:

The action, considered abstractly, has neither understanding nor will; it is not accountable, nor can it be under any moral obligation. But all these things are essential to the moral goodness which belongs to the man ...

A good action in a man is that in which he applied his intellectual powers properly, in order to judge what he ought to do, and acted according to his best judgement. This is all that can be required of a moral agent; and in this his moral goodness, in any action, consists. But is this the goodness which we ascribe to an action considered abstractly? No, surely.

... the goodness of an action, considered abstractly, can have no dependence upon the opinion or belief of an agent, any more than the truth of a proposition depends upon our believing it to be true. But, when a man exerts his active power well or ill, there is a moral goodness or turpitude, which we figuratively impute to the action, but which is truly and properly imputable to the man only; and this goodness or turpitude depends very much upon the intention of the agent, and the opinion he had of his action.

3 As Price puts it:

Liberty and *Reason* constitute the *capacity* of virtue. It is the *intention* that gives it *actual being* in a character. – The reader must not here forget the distinction before explained. To mere theoretical virtue, or (if I may so speak) the abstract reasons and fitnesses of things, praise-worthiness is not applicable. It is the actual conformity of the wills of moral agents to what they see or believe to be the fitnesses of things, that is the object of our praise and esteem. One of these may, perhaps, very properly be called the *virtue of the action*, in contradistinction from the other, which may be called the *virtue of the agent*. To the former, no particular intention is requisite; for what is *objectively* right, may be done from any motive, good or bad; and therefore, from hence alone, no merit is communicated to the agent; nay it is consistent with the greatest guilt. On the contrary, to the other the particular intention is what is most essential. When this is good, there is so far virtue, whatever is true of the *matter* of the action; for an agent, who does what is *objectively* wrong, may often be entitled to commendation. [184]

4 See Roy Lawrence's especially helpful *Motive and Intention* (Evanston: Northwestern University Press, 1972).

5 I should stress that my claim is *not* that an event, a piece of human behavior, is correctly called an action and identified *as such* only by reference to the agent's intention. No. (In fact, the view I have espoused above would be inconsistent with such a thesis. For if you identify the act that is performed wholly by reference to the agent's intention, there will be no distinction to make between the act that was intended and the act that was performed.) The situation is more complicated, though not unlike Aristotle's treatment of how acts that express some character are to be identified. Just as Aristotle requires that an act typical of some trait must be done knowingly, so we must also say that any genuine human action – as contrasted with non-voluntary behavior – must be intended. But, it does not follow that our identification of the act must be grounded in *the agent*'s conception of its nature. Rather, what we identify as the action is always grounded in a conception of what it is reasonable to believe *an* agent

would be choosing to do in such circumstances: an agent, say, who had his wits about him, understood his circumstances, and has the requisite practical experience to understand and appreciate the character and differences of the alternative courses of conduct open to him. Hence the real possibility of a disparity between the intended act and the act actually performed.

6 Descartes, *Oeuvres de Descartes*, ed. Charles Adam and Paul Tannery (Paris, 1913), II, 36. Cf. the Letter to Mersenne at I, 366, where Descartes explains that 'willing, understanding, imagining, and feeling are simply different modes of thinking, which all belong to the soul.' See Anthony Kenny's helpful discussion: 'Descartes on Ideas,' in *Descartes: A Collection of Critical Essays*, ed. Willis Doney (Garden City, N.Y.: Doubleday, 1967).

7 Cf. Descartes' *The Passions of the Soul*, Article XVIII.

8 See A. P. d'Entreves, *Natural Law: An Introduction to Legal Philosophy* (London: Hutchinson's University Library, 1951), and Aquinas, *Summa Theologica*, Quaestiones 90–97, which is available with translation in A. P. d'Entreves, *Aquinas: Selected Political Writings* (Oxford: Oxford University Press, 1948).

9 Matthew (5:48).

10 John Stuart Mill, *Utilitarianism* (Indianapolis: Bobbs-Merrill, 1971 reprint of 1861 edn).

11 Bentham's position is the same. In fact, he argues – in his usual fashion of compiling numerous examples to support his view and defeat his opponent's – that motives cannot be used to evaluate acts since no type of motive will give rise to only one kind of act. Rather, any motive can give rise to any kind of act. Identifying act and intention, he summarizes his view:

> The only way, it should seem, in which a motive can with safety be styled good or bad, is with reference to its effects in each individual instance; and principally from the intention it gives birth to: from which arise, as will be shown hereafter, the most material part of its effects. A motive is good, when the intention it gives birth to is a good one; bad, when the intention is a bad one: and an intention is good or bad, according to the material consequences that are the objects of it. So far is it from the goodness of the intention's being to be known only from the species of the motive. But from one and the same motive, as we have seen, may result intentions of every sort of complexion whatsoever.

An Introduction to the Principles of Morals and Legislation (New York: Macmillan, 1948 reprint of 1823 edn), 320.

VI   Hume and the Indirect View

1 *A Treatise of Human Nature*, ed. L. A. Selby-Bigge (London: Oxford University Press, 1968 reprint of the 1888 edn). Hereafter cited as

'*T*'. Cf. Hume's *Inquiry Concerning the Principles of Morals* (87, 96–97). Hereafter cited as '*I*'.

Rousseau, in his speculation on the historical origin of respect and esteem, is Hume's ally in this pursuit of an account of the virtues requiring reference to such a self-reflexive attitude:

> People grew accustomed to assembling in front of the huts or around a large tree; song and dance, true children of love and leisure, became the amusement or rather the occupation of idle and assembled men and women. Each began to look at the others and to want to be looked at himself, the public esteem had a value. The one who sang or danced the best, the handsomest, the strongest, the most adroit, or the most eloquent became the most highly considered; and that was the first step toward inequality ... From these preferences were born on the one hand vanity and contempt, on the other shame and envy ... *Discourse on the Origin and Foundations of Inequality* in *The First and Second Discourses*, trans. Roger D. and Judith R. Masters (New York: St. Martin's Press, 1964), 1949.

And from these preferences, essential to the social nature of man, Rousseau 'would show that to this ardor to be talked about, to this furor to distinguish oneself we owe what is best and worst among men, our virtues and vices ...' (175); 'The sociable man ... knows how to live only in the opinions of others; and it is, so to speak, from their judgement alone that he draws the sentiment of his own existence.' (179)

2 The importance of reflexive attitudes like self-respect to moral thought has recently been given considerable attention, after years of neglect. See, e.g., Thomas E. Hill, Jr., 'Servility and Self-Respect,' *The Monist*, 57 (1973), 87–104; R. S. Downie and Elizabeth Telfer, *Respect for Persons* (London: George Allen & Unwin, 1969); Stephen Darwall, 'Two Kinds of Respect,' *Ethics*, 88 (1977); Carl Cranor, 'Toward a Theory of Respect for Persons,' *American Philosophical Quarterly*, 12 (1975), 309–319; Stephen Hudson, 'The Nature of Respect,' *Social Theory and Practice*, 6 (1980), 69–90; David Sachs, 'How to Distinguish Self-Respect from Self-Esteem,' *Philosophy and Public Affairs*, 19 (1981), 346–360; Martha Nussbaum, 'Shame, Separateness, and Political Unity: Aristotle's Criticism of Plato,' in *Essays on Aristotle's Ethics*, ed. A. O. Rorty (Berkeley: University of California Press, 1980), 395–435; and the recent collection from the Tulane Conference on Respect for Persons, *Respect for Persons*, ed. O. H. Green (New Orleans: Tulane University, 1982).

3 Cf. Hume's *Inquiry Concerning the Principles of Morals*, where in the first section, Hume introduces his topic by saying '... to discover the true origin of morals ... we shall endeavor to follow a very simple method; we shall *analyze* that complication of mental qualities which form what, in common life, we call "personal merit"; and we shall consider every attribute of mind which renders a man an object either of esteem and affection or of hatred and contempt ...'.

In his *Dissertation on the Passions*, Hume refers to his considered view by noting the inseparableness of moral virtue and vice from pride and humility:

> The most probable system which has been advanced to explain the difference between vice and virtue, is, that either from a primary constitution of nature, or from a sense of public or private interest, certain characters, upon the very view and contemplation, produce uneasiness; and others, in like manner excite pleasure. The uneasiness and satisfaction, produced in the spectator, are essential to vice and virtue. To approve of a character, is to feel a delight upon its appearance. To disapprove of it, is to be sensible of an uneasiness. The pain and pleasure, therefore, being, in a manner, the primary source of blame or praise, must also be the causes of all their effects; and *consequently, the causes of pride and humility, which are the unavoidable attendants of that distinction*. (*A Dissertation on the Passions*, in *David Hume: The Philosophical Works*, ed. T. H. Green and T. H. Grose, 4 vols, Darmstadt: Scientia Verlag Aalen, 1964 reprint of 1882 edn. vol. 4, 146–147; my emphasis. Hereafter, '*D*'.)

To insure that his readers do not take him to be saying that pride is the moral sentiment, he adds in the following paragraph that 'Virtue, therefore, produces always a pleasure distinct from the pride or self-satisfaction which attends it: Vice, an uneasiness separate from the humility or remorse.'

4 There are a number of comparable passages in the *Treatise*, which I shall merely list here, for purposes of reference:

1. *T*, 473. Hume asserts that the 'pleasure' which 'is' moral approbation (i.e., the moral sentiment) arises from the apprehension of virtue *and because of the nature of virtue*, must excite pride or love.

2. *T*, 574–575. Hume reiterates the equivalence of virtue and the power of producing love or pride, vice and the power of producing humility or hatred.

3. *T*, 614. 'The pain or pleasure, which arises from the general survey of any action or quality of the mind, constitutes its vice or virtue, and gives rise to our approbation or blame, which is nothing but a fainter and more imperceptible love or hatred.'

4. *T*, 589. 'This theory may serve to explain, why the same qualities, in all cases, produce pride and love, humility and hatred; and the same man is always virtuous or vicious ... who is so to himself.'

5. *T*, 320. 'We may observe, that no person is ever prais'd by another for any quality, which wou'd not, if real, produce, of itself, a pride in the person possest of it.'

Finally, one might quarrel with my choice of the word 'self-respect.' Why not say self-esteem? Or pride? Or self-approval? My quick answer is that though Hume himself uses these other expressions as well, the nuances between them are not that great, and *present* usage of 'self-respect' conforms best to Hume's intentions. Hume recognized that there was some difficulty in naming this sentiment while preserving its ties to the not wholly secular notion of conscience that it was designed to replace: 'It seems, indeed, certain that the *sentiment* of conscious worth, the self-satisfaction proceeding from a review of a man's own conduct and character – it seems certain, I say, that this sentiment which, though the most common of all others, has no proper name in our language.' (*I*, 130)

Hume adds in a footnote:

> The term pride is commonly taken in a bad sense; but this sentiment seems indifferent, and may be either good or bad, according as it is well or ill founded, and according to the other circumstances which accompany it. The French express this sentiment by the term *amour propre*; but as they also express self-love as well as vanity by the same term, there arises a great confusion in Rouchefoucauld and many of their moral writers.

5 'Next to emulation, the greatest encourager of the noble arts is praise and glory.' 'Of the Rise and Progress of the Arts and Sciences' in *Essays Moral, Political, and Literary*, vol. III of *David Hume: The Philosophical Works*, 196. [Hereafter '*EMPL*'.] Cf. *I*, 87.

6 'The prodigious effects of education may convince us, that the mind is not altogether stubborn and inflexible, but will admit of many alterations from its original make and structure. Let a man propose to himself a model of character, which he approves: Let him keep a constant watch over himself, and bend his own mind, by a continual effort, from the vices, towards the virtues; and I doubt not but, in time, he will find, in his temper, an alteration for the better.' In 'The Sceptic' (*EMPL*, 223).

7 The notion of identification should not be intellectualized. We conceive of ourselves and others as related in certain ways, as being certain sorts of persons. We often act on these conceptions even though they typically are not given any self-conscious expression. Identification must be thought to operate in a comparable fashion. It is not something of which we are characteristically self-conscious. A young boy who identifies with some hero he watches regularly on the television, or an executive who identifies with his supervisor are good and ordinary examples. Identification is not the exercise of a capacity by a self-absorbed being, some professional dilettante of the self, who enjoys an excessive preoccupation with himself, his thoughts, his aims.

8 This fact – that when we internalize new descriptions of our self, our behavior changes as a result – is a key factor in understanding self-deception and the role it plays in creatures like ourselves.

9 *The Letters of David Hume*, ed. J. Y. T. Greig, vol. I (Oxford: Clarendon Press, 1932) [Letter 13, to Francis Hutcheson, September 1739], 32. Hereafter '*L*'. Again: 'You seem ... to embrace Dr. Butler's Opinion in his Sermons on human Nature; that our moral Sense has an Authority distinct from its Force and Durableness, & that because we always think it *ought* to prevail. But this is nothing but

an Instinct or Principle, which approves of itself upon reflection; and that is common to all of them.' [Letter 19, to Francis Hutcheson, January 1743], *L*, 47. 'Now it wou'd appear that there is a disagreeable Sympathy, as well as agreeable: And indeed, as the Sympathetic Passion is a reflex Image of the principle, it must partake of its Qualities, and be painful where that is so.' [Letter 169, to Adam Smith, July 1759], *L*, 313.

10 For a brief account of Newton's use of 'principle,' in his *Opticks*, to mean (roughly) 'ultimate character of experience,' see N. K. Smith's *The Philosophy of David Hume* (New York: St Martin's Press, 1966), 55–61.

11 *Essay on Man*, Epistle 1, 162. The four epistles of the *Essay on Man* were published successively in February, March, and May 1733, and January 1734, and quickly became a work familiar to every well-educated Englishman. Hume's account is similar to Pope's in several respects that remind us that what we all too often take as original in Hume's thought was merely a restatement of commonplace in the moral writings of the 17th and 18th century. For example, Pope expresses succinctly and with admirable flair what we often refer to as the Humean view on the relation of passions and reason:

> On Life's vast ocean diversely we sail,
> Reason the Card, but Passion is the gale.
> (Ep. 2, 107–108)

And in his account of explaining the moral as natural, he, like Hume after him, insists that 'Reason keep to Nature's road' (Ep. 2, 115) in the account of how passions can be mixed, softened, tempered, compounded, and employed to create the virtues and vices characteristic of moral life.

Pope was, to be sure, more indebted to Mandeville and less critical of him than Hume; hence a difference in tone and appearance of their characterizations of human nature. But both insist that virtues must be accounted for by natural principles, and that this account must refer to the relationship between the virtues and pride, or self-respect.

12 Cf. '... the utmost effort of human reason is to reduce the principles, productive of natural phenomena, to a greater simplicity, and to resolve the many particular effects into a few general causes, by means of reasoning from analogy, experience, and observation. But as to the general causes, we should in vain attempt their discovery ... These ultimate springs and principles are totally shut up from human curiosity' (*E*, 30).

13 *An Abstract of A Treatise of Human Nature 1740* (London: Cambridge University Press, 1938 reprint), 6.

What is the *mark* of a fundamental quality or principle, an *unexplained explainer*? Newton seemed to think that what was *not* constant and universal could not be original and ultimate; hence, its causes were to be sought, it was to be explained. This seems to be the inference he employs when he says 'Not that I affirm gravity to be essential to bodies; by their *vis insita* I mean nothing but their *vis inertiae.* This is immutable. Their gravity is diminished as they recede from the earth.' *Principia*, BK III, 'Rules of Reasoning in Philosophy.' Hume shares this assumption:

> Mankind are so much the same, in all times and places, that history informs us of nothing new or strange in this particular. Its chief use is only to discover the constant and universal principles of human nature, by showing men in all varieties of circumstances and situations, and furnishing us with material from which we may form our observations and become acquainted with the regular springs of human action and behavior. These records of wars, intrigues, factions, and revolutions, are so many collections of experiments, by which the politician or moral philosopher fixes the principles of his science ... (*E*, 83–84)

14 'It is needless to push our researches so far as to ask, why have we humanity or a fellow-feeling with others? It is sufficient that this is experienced to be a principle in human nature. We must stop somewhere in our examination of causes; and there are, in every science, some general principles beyond which we cannot hope to find any principle more general.' (*I*, 47 nt)

15 *Of The Standard of Taste*, 280. Cf. 285–290; *I*, 4, 54–55; *T*, 470–473, 574–575, 580–584, 602–603.

16 I choose this name because though Hume's account could easily be called an Ideal Observer theory, or an Impartial Spectator theory, these names already have an established currency with their (respective) connections to certain efforts in the 20th century to define ethical terms 'naturalistically,' and to Adam Smith's moral writings. Hume sometimes calls such an observer a 'judicious spectator': see, e.g., *T*, 581; cf. 591.

After many years of inept and unfair interpretation – Hume bashing was popular until the middle years of this century – this aspect of Hume's thought has received a careful and realistic appraisal. See: W. D. Falk, 'Hume on Practical Reason,' *Philosophical Studies*, 27 (1975), 1–18, and 'Hume on Is and Ought,' *Canadian Journal of Philosophy*, 6 (1976), 359–378; Pall S. Ardal, *Passion and Value in Hume's Treatise* (Edinburgh: Edinburgh University Press, 1966); David F. Norton, *David Hume: Common-Sense Moralist, Sceptical Metaphysician* (Princeton: Princeton University Press, 1982), 107–120; D. D. Raphael, 'The Impartial Spectator,' *Proceedings of the British Academy*, 58 (1972), 3–22; Peter Jones, 'Cause, Reason, and Objectivity in Hume's Aesthetics,' in *Hume: A Re-evaluation*, ed. J. T. King and D. Livingston (New York: Fordham University Press, 1976); and J. T. King, 'The Place of the Language of Morals in Hume's Second Enquiry,' in *Hume: A Re-evaluation*.

17 'Actions are not virtuous nor vicious; but only so far as they are proofs of certain Qualitys or durable Principles in the Mind. This is a Point I shou'd have establish'd more expressly than I have done ... tis on the Goodness or Badness of the Motives that the Virtue of

the Action depends. This proves, that to every virtuous action there must be a Motive or impelling Passion distinct from the Virtue, & that Virtue can never be the sole Motive to any Action' [Letter 13, to Francis Hutcheson, September, 1739], *L*, 34–35. Cf. *T*, 592, 603.

Hutcheson, of course, shared this view that the object of moral consciousness, or the moral sense, is not conduct *simply*: 'The Quality approved by our moral Sense is conceived to reside in the Person approved, and to be a Perfection and Dignity in him ... The admired Quality is conceived as the Perfection of the Agent ...' *An Inquiry into the Original of our Ideas of Beauty and Virtue* (Farnborough: Gregg International Publishers, 1969 reprint of the fourth edition of 1738), 130. As did Shaftesbury, who made it the centerpiece of distinguishing moral from nonmoral value: 'But to proceed from what is esteemed mere goodness, and lies within the reach and capacity of all sensible creatures, to that which is called virtue or merit, and is allowed to man only. In a creature capable of forming general notions of things, not only the outward beings which offer themselves to the sense are the objects of affection, but the actions themselves, and the affections of pity, kindness, gratitude, and their contraries, being brought by the mind into reflection, become objects. So that, by means of this reflected sense, there arises another kind of affection towards those very affections themselves, which have already been felt, and are now become the subject of a new liking or dislike.' *An Inquiry Concerning Virtue or Merit*, Book I, Part II, Section I. First corrected and authorized edition printed in *Characteristics of Men, Manners, Opinions, Times* (Indianapolis: Bobbs-Merrill, 1964 reprint of 1711 edn).

VII   The Dualism of Humean Virtues

1 Cf. *T*, xxi, and *An Abstract of a Treatise of Human Nature*, 6. At *T*, 282, Hume compares this principle of parsimony's application in natural and moral philosophy:

> Besides, we find in the course of nature, that tho' the effects be many, the principles, from which they arise, are commonly but few and simple, and that 'tis the sign of an unskilful naturalist to have recourse to a different quality, in order to explain every different operation ...
>
> Here, therefore, moral philosophy is in the same condition as natural, with regard to astronomy before the time of Copernicus. The antients, tho' sensible of that maxim, *that nature does nothing in vain*, contriv'd such intricate systems of the heavens, as seemed inconsistent with true philosophy, and gave place at last to something more simple and natural. To invent without scruple a new principle to every new phaenomenon ... [is] certain proof[s], that none of these principles is the just one ...

Hume is, of course, following his chartered course to apply the new experimental approach to morals. Newton's first dictate in his 'Rules of Reasoning in Philosophy,' *Principia* (Book III) was:

> *We are to admit no more causes of natural things than such as are both true and sufficient to explain their appearances.*
>
> To this purpose the philosophers say that Nature does nothing in vain, and more is in vain when less will serve; for Nature is pleased with simplicity, and affects not the pomp of superfluous causes.

2 Cf. *I*, 88–89.

3 Cf. '... but for this very reason it is necessary for us, in our calm judgements and discourse concerning the characters of men, to neglect all these differences and render our sentiments more public and social. Besides that we ourselves often change our situation in this particular; we every day meet with persons who are in a situation different from us, and who could never converse with us were we to remain constantly in that position and point of view which is peculiar to ourselves. The intercourse of sentiments, therefore, in society and conversation makes us form some general unalterable standard by which we may approve or disapprove of characters and manners.' *I*, 55–56.

4 *T*, 316–317, my emphasis. Cf. *T*, 321, 575–576, 589; *DP*, 152, 155.

5 Sympathy does enable us to see and feel what it is like to be someone else; but it does not merely enliven our understanding of others and what their life is like, as seen from a perspective internal to that life. *It enables us to feel, not merely what others feel, but as humans do*: to have feelings, attitudes, emotions, and sentiments that are *shareable*. The power of sympathy permits us to feel what others feel because *we could not feel the way we do* unless we could, in Hume's sense, sympathize with others: participate in an 'intercourse of sentiments' that makes possible *the very sentiments* we identify ourselves and others as possessing.

This matter will be explored in more detail when we examine the 'steady and general point of view' that secures the agreement necessary for such discourse. See Chapter VIII.

6 '[man's] very first state and situation may justly be esteem'd social. This, however, hinders not, but that philosophers may, if they please, extend their reasoning to the suppos'd *state of nature*; provided they allow it to be a mere philosophical fiction, which never had, and never cou'd have any reality.' (*T*, 493) cf. *I*, 35.

7 Cf. 'Scarce any human action is entirely complete in itself or is performed without reference to the actions of others, which are requisite to make it answer fully the intention of the agent.' (*E*, 98) Cf. *I*, 55–56.

8 'Human nature cannot, by any means, subsist without the association of individuals.' *I*, 35.

9 Hence Hume's insistence that 'It is ... on opinion only that government is founded.' 'On the First Principles of Government,' *EMPL*, 29. The power and effectiveness of government can only be explained

by opinion – the result of persisting customs and mutual expectations sanctified by time. How could it otherwise be that the few, with so little strength in their numbers, could govern the many?

Current utility (expected mutual benefit) of conventions, to which reference is appropriate for their justification, must be distinguished from their historical origins. As Hume puts the matter in discussing the development of the apparatus of government in his 'Of the Origin of Government': 'But though this progress of human affairs may appear certain and inevitable, and though the support which allegiance brings to justice, be founded on obvious principles of human nature, it cannot be expected that men should beforehand be able to discover them, or foresee their operation. Government commences more casually and more imperfectly.' *EMPL*, 115. Cf. 'A long course of time, with a variety of accidents and circumstances, are requisite to produce those great revolutions, which so much diversify the face of human affairs.' 'Of Commerce,' *EMPL*, 292.

10 Both custom and sympathy are psychological principles that Hume regards as immensely powerful. 'Custom has two *original* effects upon the mind, in bestowing a *facility* in the performance of any action or the conception of any object; and afterwards a tendency or inclination towards it.' (*T*, 422) It is 'so powerful as even to convert pain into pleasure, and give us a relish, in time for what at first was most harsh and disagreeable.' (*T*, 423) Sympathy also has this power: see *T*, 589.

11 'From the apparent usefulness of the social virtues it has readily been inferred by skeptics, both ancient and modern, that all moral distinctions arise from education, and were at first invented, and afterwards encouraged, by the art of politicians in order to render men tractable and subdue their natural ferocity and selfishness, which incapacitated them for society. This principle, indeed, of precept and education must so far be owned to have a powerful influence that it may frequently increase or diminish, beyond their natural standard, the sentiments of approbation or dislike ... But that *all* moral affection or dislike arise from this origin will never surely be allowed by any judicious inquirer. Had nature made no such distinction, founded on the original constitution of the mind, the words *honorable* and *shameful*, *lovely*, and *odious*, *noble* and *despicable* had never had any place in any language, nor could politicians, had they invented these terms, even have been able to render them intelligible or make them convey any idea to the audience.' *I*, 42.

12 See, e.g., *T*, 281.

13 Cf. 'in vain sho'd we expect to find, in *uncultivated nature*, a remedy to this inconvenience; or hope for any inartificial principle of the human mind, which might control those partial affections, and make us overcome the temptations arising from our circumstances. The idea of justice can never serve this purpose, or be taken for a natural principle, capable of inspiring men with an equitable conduct towards each other.' (*T*, 488)

14 'You sometimes, in my Opinion, ascribe the Original of Property & Justice to public Benevolence, & sometimes to private Benevolence

towards the Possessors of the Goods, neither of which seem to me satisfactory. ... You are so much afraid to derive anything of Virtue from Artifice or human Conventions, that you have neglected what seems to me the most satisfactory Reason, viz lest near Relations, having so many Opportunities in their Youth, might debauch each other, if the least Encouragement or Hope was given to these Desires, or if they were not early represst by an artificial Horror, inspird against them.' [Letter 19, to Francis Hutcheson, 1743], *L*, 47–48.

15 Hume insisted that writers like Mandeville, who claimed that justice was artificial, in the sense of being *wholly* a matter of social convention without any regard to human nature and its constraints, had gone too far:

> the matter has been carry'd too far by certain writers on morals, who seem to have employ'd their utmost efforts to extirpate all sense of virtue from among mankind. Any artifice of politicians may assist nature in the producing of those sentiments, which she suggests to us, and may even on some occasions, produce alone an approbation or esteem for any particular action; but 'tis impossible it should be the sole cause of the distinction we make betwixt vice and virtue. ... The utmost politicians can perform, is, to extend the natural sentiments beyond their original bounds; but still nature must furnish the materials, and give us some notion of moral distinctions.' (*T*, 500)

It is a crucial aspect of Hume's account that the artificial can never replace the natural, only extend or redirect it:

> All this is the effect of the natural and inherent principles and passions of human nature; and as these passions and principles are inalterable, it may be thought, that our conduct, which depends upon them, must be so too, and that 'twou'd be in vain, either for moralists or politicians, to tamper with us ... All they can pretend to do is give a new direction to those natural passions, and teach us that we can better satisfy our appetites in an oblique and artificial manner, than by their headlong and impetuous motion. (*T*, 521)

16 Hence the familiar division of the *Inquiry* into a discussion of qualities useful (to ourselves or others) and those that are immediately agreeable (to ourselves or others): the *utile* and the *dulce*.

17 Cf. [Letter 13, to Francis Hutcheson, September 1739], *L*, 34–35.

18 *T*, 478.

19 Cf. *T*, 579–580.

20 When therefore men have had enough experience to observe, that whatever may be the consequence of any single act of justice, perform'd by a single person, yet the whole system of actions, concurr'd by the whole society, is infinitely advantageous to the whole, and to every part; it is not long before justice and property take place. Every member of society is sensible of this interest ... And thus justice establishes itself by a kind of convention or

agreement; that is, by a sense of interest, suppos'd to be common to all, and where every single act is perform'd in expectation that others are to perform the like. Without such a convention, no one wou'd ever have dream'd, that there was such a virtue as justice, or have been induc'd to conform his action to it. Taking any single act, my justice may be pernicious in every respect; and 'tis only upon the supposition, that others are to imitate my example, that I can be induc'd to embrace that virtue; since nothing but this combination can render justice advantageous, or afford me any motives to conform myself to its rules. (*T*, 498)

In the absence of general conformity to the conventions that co-ordinate and stabilize, we have no motive to conform to these conventions. It follows that artificial virtues are not virtues in the absence of such general conformity – something about which I believe Hume is right. But this also seems to lead to another difference between natural and artificial virtues: for motives to perform acts of natural virtues would seem to exist when motives to perform acts of artificial virtues would not.

21 '*Thus self-interest is the original motive to the establishment of justice; but a sympathy with public interest is the source of moral approbation that attends the virtue.*' (*T*, 499–500)
22 *Treatise*, Book III, Part III.

VIII   Moral Points of View

1 Cf. *T*, 497. John Rawls, 'Two Concepts of Rules,' *Philosophical Review*, 64 (1955), 3–32.
2 See, e.g., *T*, 484–516; *I*, 14–40.
3 'Trade was never esteemed an affair of state until the last century; and there scarcely is any ancient writer on politics, who has made mention of it.' 'Of Civil Liberty,' *EMPL*, 157.
4 'Of Commerce,' *EMPL*, 288–289.
5 *I*, 124.
6 *I*, 55–56, my emphasis. Cf. *I*, 93–94, 124. Hume adds in a footnote that:

It is wisely ordained by nature that private connections should commonly prevail over universal views and considerations, otherwise our actions and affections would be dissipated and lost for want of a *proper limited object*. Thus a small benefit done to ourselves, or our near friends, excites more lively sentiments of love and approbation than a great benefit done to a distant commonwealth; but we still know here, as in all senses, to correct these inequalities by reflection, and retain a general standard of vice and virtue, founded chiefly on general usefulness. (my emphasis)

Hume is, I think, uneasily aware that his account requires not just

141

that the moral sentiment have as its object a so-called *universal* object – say, the interests of everyone, where such interests are considered on analogy with viewing not just one cat, but rather all cats – but an *abstract* object: say, the interests of everyone alike. Of course the latter is not a 'proper limited object.'

7 Something that can be guaranteed only by some means such as making you indistinguishable from anyone else: an anonymous anyone.

8 *I*, 122. Notice that Hume does *not* say that *from within* such a point of view such considerations are recognized as morally relevant, but outweighed by the balance of good that comes from rules that ignore them. (He uses such an argument for employing a view so characterized.) From within, *such* balancing is a mistake: there is nothing to balance.

9 See, e.g., Bernard Williams' most helpful discussion of this so-called Kantian element in his 'Persons, Character and Morality,' in his *Moral Luck* (Cambridge: Cambridge University Press, 1981), 1–19.

10 See Hume's detailed commentary on this example at *T*, 518–519.

11 *T*, 481, my emphasis.

12 Hume is clearly indebted to Butler, who advanced a comparable 'naturalness principle' in his *Fifteen Sermons Preached at Rolls Chapel*:

> There are two ways in which the subject of morals may be treated. One begins from inquiring into the abstract relations of things; the other from a matter of fact, namely, what the particular nature of man is, its several parts, their economy or constitution; from whence it proceeds to determine what course of life it is, which is correspondent to this whole nature.
>
> The following discourses proceed chiefly in this latter method. The three first wholly. They were intended to explain what is meant by the nature of man, when it is said that virtue consists in following, and vice in deviating from it ... [Paragraphs 12 and 13, 'The Preface'], *Five Sermons* (Indianapolis: Bobbs-Merrill, 1950 reprint of 1726 edn). Cf. *I*, 8, where Hume follows Butler in drawing this very same distinction.

13 *T*, 483–484. Cf.

> as every immortality is deriv'd from some defect or unsoundness of the passions ... 'twill be easy to know, whether we be guilty of any immorality, with regard to others, by considering the *natural*, and usual force of those several affections, which are directed towards them. Now it appears, that in the original frame of mind, our strongest attention is confin'd to ourselves; our next is extended to relations and acquaintance; and 'tis only the weakest that reaches strangers and indifferent persons. This partiality, then, and unequal affection, must not only have an intimate influence on our behavior and conduct in society but even on our ideas of vice and virtue; so as to make us regard *any remarkable transgression of such a degree of partiality, either by too great an*

enlargement, or contraction of the affections, as vicious and immoral.
This we may observe in our common judgements concerning
actions, where we blame a person, who centers all his affections in
his family, or is so regardless of them, as, in any opposition of
interest, to give preference to a stranger, or mere chance
acquaintance. From all which it follows, that our natural
uncultivated ideas of morality, instead of providing a remedy for
the partiality of affections, do rather conform themselves to that
partiality, and give it additional force and influence. (*T*, 488–489;
my emphasis)

Why is justice, the rules of property that require us to ignore the
objects of our 'partial' affections, not thought to be 'too great an
enlargement'?

14 See *T*, 481, 484f, 586.
15 See *T*, 518–519, 521–523, 619–620.
16 My understanding of Hume and the depth of his attempt at an 'internal' and secular justification has been enriched by Alasdair MacIntyre's work in two different ways. First, by his sympathetic treatment
of Hume in his 'Hume on "Is" and "Ought",' in V. Chappell, ed.
Hume (South Bend, Indiana: University of Notre Dame Press, 1966),
and second, by his account of the project of justification and his harsh
treatment of Hume in his more recent *After Virtue*.
17 [Letter 13, to Francis Hutcheson, Sept. 1739], *L*, 33. Cf. [Letter 3,
to Dr George Cheyne, 1734], *L*, 16.
18 [Letter 19, to Francis Hutcheson, January 1743], *L*, 47.
19 Cf. 'Habits more than reason we find in everything to be the governing principle of mankind.' *The History of Great Britain: The Reign
of James I and Charles I* (Harmondsworth: Penguin Books, 1970),
259.
20 Butler conceived conscience as the moral faculty which recognizes
the absolute binding nature of moral principles: an inner voice that
demands unconditional supremacy over all springs of action. Hume,
while rejecting this view and the argument that buttressed it, found
something worthwhile in Butler's arguments: namely, that *the 'originality' of a principle provides it with legitimacy since it indicates that it
is a fundamental part of human nature*: hence, we find here the connection between 'originality' and the naturalness principle, the principle that requires morality to respect our natural affections. What
Hume explicitly rejected was Butler's thesis that 'original' principles,
such as conscience, are original because they are part of the design
according to which our nature has been constructed.
21 Hence the view of modern liberals of a Kantian bent – that, for
example, when moral considerations of justice clash with other moral
considerations, such as those arising from personal relationships, considerations of justice always take precedence – is not Hume's. Natural
and artificial virtues are, for him, interdependent.
22 Hume is also often credited with talk about *adopting* the moral point
of view. This is not his language; he speaks of 'moves' from one point

of view to another, as for instance, when he describes the 'move' from a 'private' perspective to a 'steady and general' one. In any case, if a choice to employ this language is made, it should carry with it the warning that *adoption* of any point of view is not a matter of choice. It is just a fact about us that we employ the moral point of view: 'The fabric and constitution of our mind no more depends on our choice, than that of our body.' 'The Sceptic,' *EMPL*, 221. The questions that remain are why we do so, whether we are justified in doing so, and what it is that we so employ.

23 See, e.g., *T*, 471–473, 580–582, 589–591; *ST*, 285–292.

24 *I*, 122. Cf. *T*, 532–533.

25 'In order to pave the way for such a sentiment [a principle of taste] and give a proper discernment of its object, it is often necessary, we find, that much reasoning should precede, that nice distinctions be made, just conclusions drawn, distant comparisons formed, complicated relations examined, and general facts fixed and ascertained.' *I*, 6.

Again: 'When the critic has no delicacy, he judges without any distinction, and is only affected by the grosser and palpable qualities of the object: The finer touches pass unnoticed and disregarded. Where he is not aided by practice, his verdict is attended with confusion and hesitation. Where no comparison has been employed, the most frivolous beauties, such as rather merit the name of defects, are the object of his admiration. Where he lies under the influence of prejudice, all his natural sentiments are perverted.' *ST*, 288–289.

And: '. . . with regard to the sciences and liberal arts, a fine taste is, in some measure, the same with strong sense, or at least depends so much upon it that they are inseparable. In order to judge aright of a composition of genius, there are so many views to be taken in, so many circumstances to be compared, and such a knowledge of human nature is requisite, that no man, who is not possessed of the soundest judgement, will ever make a tolerable critic in such performances.' 'Of Delicacy of Taste and Passion,' *EMPL*, 93. Cf. *I*, 108–109; *ST*, 274–276, 278–280.

26 All passions and sentiments that are durable must be confirmed by sympathy: see, e.g., *T*, 316, 321, 589; *DP*, 151–152.

27 Hume's descriptions of a 'move' to a steady and general viewpoint are not entirely happy. If, as I have argued, all sentiments, both moral and nonmoral, must be socially confirmed or utterly fleeting, there is no perspective from which one moves: the solipsism of the sentiments that Hume deplores and condemns, where each person's sentiments and judgements refer only to his 'peculiar' situation, is not even intelligible. The 'peculiar' and 'private' features he mentions are intelligible only because they are the *result* of a deviation from shared judgements; they are not a basis for a move to shared judgements. The solipsistic viewpoint can be expressed only because one's consciousness of oneself, as an individual, is made possible through social relations with others. The power of sympathy – to enable us to have the shareable sentiments we do, to feel the very

way we do – makes possible sentiments from which there can be deviations of the sort Hume mentioned.

28 The canonical interpretation of Hume's account incorrectly imposes a Kantian structure on Hume's thought. It holds that one assumes the 'steady and general' point of view from which we should make moral judgements through a series of *abstractions* from our own 'peculiar' point of view: to eliminate subjective and personal considerations we are to exclude information about ourselves, we abstract from our relation to the object of evaluation, and so forth. But as I show below, Hume demands an *enlargement* of our 'peculiar' point of view, not an abstraction from it, to arrive at a shared communal point of view.

29 See, e.g., John Rawls, *A Theory of Justice* (Cambridge: Harvard University Press, 1971), 136–142; Stephen Darwall, 'Is There a Kantian Foundation for Rawlsian Justice?,' in *John Rawls' Theory of Social Justice*, ed. H. Blocker and E. Smith (Athens: Ohio University Press, 1980).

The idea of a veil of ignorance, simply put, represents the notion of device that filters or screens information to promote impartial consideration of some object of evaluation. Kant's veil functions to hide much from view in the Kingdom of Ends: '. . . if we abstract from the personal difference of rational beings and thus from all content of their private ends . . .' (*Foundations of the Metaphysics of Morals* (Indianapolis: Bobbs-Merrill, 1959 reprint of 1785 edn), 51, *Ak.* [433].)

30 A will is truly free when and only when it is free from any ground of determination in nature. Only, that is, when it obeys its own dictates; only when reason, represented as a rational will, determines itself, is self-grounding:

Since the mere form of law can be thought only by reason and is consequently not an object of the senses and therefore does not belong among appearances, the conception of this form as the determining ground of the will is distinct from all determining grounds of events in nature according to the law of causality, for these grounds must themselves be appearances. Now, as no determining ground of the will except universal legislative form can serve as a law for it, such a will must be conceived as wholly independent of the natural law of appearances in their mutual relations, i.e., the law of causality. Such independence is called *freedom* in the strictest, i.e., transcendental, sense. Therefore, a will to which only the legislative form of the maxim can serve is a free will. (*Critique of Practical Reason*, tr. L. W. Beck (Indianapolis: Bobbs-Merrill, 1956 reprint of 1788 edn), 28; *Ak.* [28–29].)

31 . . . in judging of characters, the only interest or pleasure, which appears the same to every spectator, is that of the person himself, whose character is examin'd; or that of persons who have a connexion with him. And tho' such interests and pleasures touch

145

us more faintly than our own, yet being more constant and universal, they counter-balance the latter even in practice, and are alone admitted in speculation as the standard of virtue and morality. They alone produce the particular feeling or sentiment, on which moral distinctions depend. (*T*, 591)

At least one reason for insisting that it is through sympathy with a person's close circle that an evaluator's partiality is overcome is that the principle of sympathy has different effects at different distances: we sympathize more with persons contiguous to us. So sympathy with the object of evaluation could not take us as far out of ourselves as is required for a 'steady and general' viewpoint. But Hume is also claiming, implicitly, that the role of sympathy in passion confirmation is sufficiently strong to create such a point of view wherever a close circle, or its enlargement, can be formed: anyone in the circle has sufficient commerce with other members to assure that their sentiments are not 'peculiar' to themselves.

This account seems inadequate, as it stands, on several points. First, Hume fails to address here problems such as *shared* prejudices and misunderstandings, which would not be corrected. Second, if sympathy does not work well at a distance, a sympathetic sharing with a person's close circle is unlikely to provide the needed gain when both the person (being evaluated) and his close circle are equally distant.

32 In my 'Right Reason and Mortal Gods,' *The Monist*, 66 (1983), 134–143, I locate several different factors in Hobbes' thought that contribute to the claim that there must be such a common point of view.

IX Reflections on the Nature of the Beast

1 Again, while Hume maintains that such partiality of natural affection places limits on moral thought – that our ideas of virtue and vice are given additional force and influence by recognizing its legitimate role – he uses these very facts to establish that justice is not a natural virtue, at the same time almost undercutting the basis of the contrast by pointing to considerations that weigh in against his verdict on the value of natural affection:

Here are two persons, who dispute an estate; of whom one is rich, a fool, and a batchelor; the other, poor, a man of sense, and has a numerous family: The first is my enemy; the second my friend. Whether I be actuated in this affair by a view to public or private interest, by friendship or enmity, I must be induc'd to do my utmost to procure the estate of the latter. Nor wou'd any consideration of the right and property of the persons be able to restrain me, were I actuated only by natural motives, without any combination or convention with others. For as all property depends on the ordinary course of our passions and actions; and as these are only directed by particular motives; 'tis evident, such a partial conduct must be suitable to the strictest morality, and cou'd never be a violation of property. Were men, therefore, to take the liberty of acting with regard to the laws of society, as they do in every other affair ... this wou'd produce an infinite confusion in human society, and that the avidity and partiality of men wou'd quickly bring disorder into the world, if not restrain'd by some general and inflexible principles. 'Twas, therefore, with a view to this inconvenience, that men have establish'd those principles, which are *unchangeable by spite and favour, and by particular views of private or public interest.* These rules, then, are artificially invented from a certain purpose, and *are contrary to the common principles of human nature,* which accommodate themselves to circumstances, and have no stated invariable method of operation. (*T*, 532–533; my emphasis)

2 Hume is wrong to think that there is a *secure* or a *fixed* (timeless) starting point for the account possessing such a quality. He is, as I remarked earlier, much too confident that we can correctly and easily identify which passions are natural, and use them as our starting point. But there is no privileged access to what is natural; when, for example, we sort motives as natural or artificial, our classifications are a reflection of our refined moral sensibilities: the very sensibilities that are the object of explanation. Hume should have said that the role of natural passions in his theory is like the role of particular moral cases in Aristotle's: each (in their respective theories) provides the principal, though not the sole, grounds for discovering general moral principles. Properly understood, the general principles explain the particular cases, even though the particular cases qualify and limit the general principles just as the general principles qualify and limit them. The naturalness of a principle is a sign that it is of a type which is a principal source of our moral conceptions; but principles of this type are not the touchstone of the moral order because they are natural.

3 See my 'The Nature of Respect,' *Social Theory and Practice*, 6 (1980), 80–88.

4 The Stoic tradition of Natural Law, as transmitted to the Scottish Enlightenment through the authority of Cicero, was canonized in Scots Law: see A. L. Macfie, 'The Scottish Tradition in Economic Thought,' in *The Individual in Society: Essays on Adam Smith* (London: Allen & Unwin, 1967), 19–41; R. L. Emerson, 'Scottish Universities in the Eighteenth Century, 1690–1800,' *Studies in Voltaire and the Eighteenth Century*, 167 (1977), 453–473; Ronald Cant, 'Origins of the Enlightenment in Scotland: the Universities', in R. H. Campbell and Andrew Skinner, *The Origins and Nature of the Scottish Enlightenment* (Edinburgh: John Donald Publishers, 1982), 42–64; Peter Stein, 'The Influence of Roman Law on the Law of Scotland,' *The Juridical Review*, 8 N.S. (1963), 204–245.

For helpful studies of the works of Gershom Carmichael, the first occupant of the Chair of Moral Philosophy at the University of Glasgow – the chair subsequently assumed by Francis Hutcheson and later Adam Smith – who played a crucial role in establishing the natural jurisprudence tradition in Scottish universities and introduced Pufendorf into the curriculum, see: James Moore and Michael Silverthorne, 'Natural Sociability and Natural Rights in the Moral Philosophy of Gerschom Carmichael,' in V. Hope ed. *Philosophers of the Scottish Enlightenment* (Edinburgh: Edinburgh University Press, 1984), 1–12, and 'Gershom Carmichael and the Natural Jurisprudence Tradition in Eighteenth Century Scotland,' in Roger Emerson, *Man and Nature* (London, Ontario: University of Western Ontario, 1982), 41–54.

5 See Duncan Forbes' careful and most helpful account of Hume's relation to Natural Law in his *Hume's Philosophical Politics* (Cambridge: Cambridge University Press, 1975), 3–36, and 'Natural Law and the Scottish Enlightenment,' *The Origins and Nature of the Scottish Enlightenment* (Edinburgh: John Donald Publishers, 1982), 186–204.

6 There is 'one law, eternal and unchangeable binding at all times on all people.' *De Republica*, III, xxii, tr. G. Sabine & S. Smith (Indianapolis: Bobbs-Merrill), 216; cf. *De Officiis*, I, xxx; III, v–vi, tr. T. Cockman (London: Routledge, 1894).

7 *E*, 83; cf. *T*, 537 and:

> All this is the effect of the natural and inherent principles and passions of human nature; and as these passions and principles are inalterable, it may be thought, that our conduct, which depends upon them, must be so too, and that 'twou'd be in vain, either for moralists or politicians, to tamper with us . . . All they can pretend to do is give a new direction to those natural passions, and teach us that we can better satisfy our appetites in an oblique and artificial manner, than by their headlong and impetuous motion. (*T*, 521)

8 Cf. '. . . the common principles of human nature . . . accommodate themselves to circumstances and have no stated invariable method of operation' [as the principles of justice do]. *T*, 533.

9 That Hume's training in law affected his judgement is not in doubt; but here it doubtlessly received support from his assumption, borrowed from Newton and others, that ultimate principles must be *constant* and *universal*. [See the prior discussion in Chapter VI.]

10 See, e.g., *A Dialogue*, published originally in the first edition of the *Enquiry* in 1751, and reprinted in *I*, 141–158, where Hume scornfully condemns the practical implementation of philosophical enthusiasm. Cf. Hume's apprehension of how metaphysical conceptions obscure, falsify, or prevent accurate perceptions: 'And it seems a reasonable presumption that systems and hypotheses have perverted our natural understanding when a theory so simple and obvious could so long have escaped the most elaborate examination.' (*I*, 90)

X Epilogue: Morality and Human Character

1 Although I have argued that Kant should be understood as an advocate of the Indirect View, it is easy to see how he is commonly regarded as a supporter of the Direct. For instance, if you say that we should take the best of Kant's thought and make what we can with it – a common reconstructivist move – and then proceed to reject entirely the transcendental psychology and its connection to the Kantian account of the relationship between autonomy and reason, the disemboweled result will often be a version of the Direct View: a type of decision procedure for determining whether acts or kinds of acts are morally permissible or not.

  And there is *something* right about interpreting Kant along such lines: namely, that Kant wanted his theoretical machinery to be employed to *direct* action, to bring about a just moral order through the application of theory to guide agents in what choices they should make. Plainly, this is a central belief shared by advocates of the Direct View. Nonetheless, the reduction of Kant's moral thought to a procedure or set of procedures for action guidance leaves unexplained the justification for the decision procedure; that is just one indication of the unsoundness of such a reconstruction.

2 See, e.g., C. D. Broad, *Five Types of Ethical Theory* (London: Oxford University Press, 1930), 116; D. D. Raphael, *The Moral Sense* (London: Oxford University Press, 1947), 97.

3 *I*, 91.

4 If we are such complex creatures, would a life that eliminated much of that complexity make us better off? This is a hard question that I cannot pretend to answer. But, once raised, it does not seem obvious that the embodiment of this conception of rationality in a harmony of design is something we should prefer.

5 This premise will be discussed more fully in Section 2 when we address the naturalness principle.

6 Much to my delight I find that Bentham is an important ally here:

> Perfect happiness belongs to the imaginary regions of philosophy,
> and must be classed with the universal elixir and the
> philosopher's stone. In the age of greatest perfection, fire will
> burn, tempests will rage, man will be subject to infirmity, to
> accidents, and to death. It may be possible to diminish the
> influence of, but not to destroy, the sad and mischievous passions.
> The unequal gifts of nature and of fortune will create jealousies:
> there will always be oppositions of interests; and, consequently,
> rivalries and hatred. Pleasures will be purchased by pains;
> enjoyments by privations. Painful labor, daily subjection, a
> condition nearly allied to indigence, will always be the lot of
> numbers. . . .
>   This faithful picture, the result of facts, is more worthy of
> regard than the deceptive exaggerations which excite our hopes

149

for a moment, and then precipitate us into discouragement, as if we had deceived ourselves in hoping for happiness. Let us seek only for what is attainable: it presents a career sufficiently vast for genius; sufficiently difficult for the exercise of the greatest virtues. [Jeremy Bentham, 'Essay on the Influence of Time and Place in Matters of Legislation,' in *The Works of Jeremy Bentham*, ed. John Bowring (New York: Russell & Russell, 1962), vol. 1, 194]

7 The scope of the issues that arise under this general conflict is vast, including issues such as the prescription of placebos, restriction of diet, withholding of information to procure consent for medically necessary treatment or diagnostic measures, small lies to foster hope, and so on. The literature on paternalism in medicine is vast. A selective sample that provides an overview: Earl Shelp, ed. *Beneficence and Health Care* (Dordrecht, Holland: D. Reidel Publishing Co., 1982); Tom Beauchamp and James Childress, *Principles of Biomedical Ethics*, 2nd edn (New York: Oxford University Press, 1983); Charles Culver and Bernard Gert, *Philosophy in Medicine: Conceptual and Ethical Issues in Medicine and Psychiatry* (New York: Oxford University Press, 1982); Alexander Capron, 'Informed Consent in Catastrophic Disease Research and Treatment,' *University of Pennsylvania Law Review*, 123 (1974), 364–376; C. H. Fellner and J. R. Marshall, 'Kidney Donors: The Myth of Informed Consent,' *American Journal of Psychiatry*, 126 (1970), 1245–1251; Franz Ingelfinger, 'Arrogance,' *New England Journal of Medicine*, 303 (1980), 1507–1511; James Childress, *Who Should Decide?: Paternalism in Health Care* (New York: Oxford University Press, 1982); Wade L. Robison and Michael S. Pritchard, eds, *Medical Responsibility: Paternalism, Informed Consent, and Euthanasia* (Clifton, N.J.: Humana Press, 1979).

8 Here, and throughout this chapter, my ideas have been focused helpfully by Stephen Darwall's sympathetic and insightful defense of a Kantian perspective on the nature of morality and rationality in his *Impartial Reason* (Ithaca: Cornell University Press, 1983).

9 That nature, in this sense, must be refined is a matter about which Hume was clear: 'Wherever nature has given the mind a propensity to any vice, or to any passion disagreeable to others, refined breeding has taught men to throw the biass on the opposite side, and to preserve, in all their behavior, the appearance of sentiments different from those to which they naturally inclined.' 'Of the Rise and Progress of the Arts and Sciences,' *EMPL*, 192.

10 See, e.g., E. Zeller, *The Stoics, Epicureans and Sceptics* (London: Longmans, Green & Co., 1892), 226f.

11 The attribution of this premise to his rationalist predecessors is, of course, crucial to many of Hume's arguments against them: see, e.g., *T*, 456–468.

12 The Kantian Kingdom of Ends could be thought of as the merger of the Stoic cosmopolis and the medieval Kingdom of God. This, it seems to me, is one way to bring out the role of Reason, for Kant, as

a surrogate for the role God played in previous thought. For the Stoic, man's end was provided by Nature; for the medieval Christian, by God; for Kant, by Reason. That Hume's moral thought consistently refused to rely, consciously or unconsciously, explicitly or implicitly, on such a conception of a Deity or some substitute makes it the first systematic moral theory that is truly secular and modern.

13 Hence implicit in such pursuits for the moral point of view is a conception of morality that guides the project: morality is *about timeless* truths or ideas. This, in turn, characterizes the fear.

14 The numbers engaged in such pursuits speak to the power of this idea and the ideal of metaphysical perfection that underlies it. The automatic and inordinate value we place, or tend to place, on permanence and eternalness says something about us.

15 *Foundations of the Metaphysics of Morals*, tr. L. W. Beck (Indianapolis: Bobbs-Merrill, 1959 reprint of 1785 edn), 5; *Ak.*, [389].

16 See, e.g., the work of Kuhn, Lakatos, Hanson, Quine, Sellars, Davidson and Rorty to name a few.

17 As Rawls puts it in his *A Theory of Justice*: 'the point of view from which noumenal selves see the world.' (255)

18 Such a purge, to obtain a sure grounding for morality, is the moral analogue of the Cartesian purge of the mind to insure a firm grounding for knowledge.

Bibliography

———◆———

Anscombe, G. E. M. 'Modern Moral Philosophy.' *Philosophy* 33 (1958).

Anscombe, G. E. M. 'On Brute Facts.' *Analysis* 18 (1958).

Ardal, Pall S. *Passion and Value in Hume's Treatise.* Edinburgh: Edinburgh University Press, 1966.

Aristotle. *The Works of Aristotle. Vol. IX. Ethica Nicomachea.* Translated by W. D. Ross. London: Oxford University Press, 1966.

Baron, Marcia. 'The Alleged Repugnance of Acting From Duty.' *Journal of Philosophy* 81 (1984).

Beauchamp, Tom and Childress, James. *Principles of Biomedical Ethics.* 2nd edn, New York: Oxford University Press, 1983.

Bentham, Jeremy. *An Introduction to the Principles of Morals and Legislation.* New York: Macmillan, 1948 reprint of 1823 edn.

Bentham, Jeremy. 'Essay on the Influence of Time and Place in Matters of Legislation.' *The Works of Jeremy Bentham.* Edited by John Bowring. New York: Russell & Russell, 1962.

Blum, Lawrence. *Friendship, Altruism and Morality.* London: Routledge & Kegan Paul, 1980.

Brandt, Richard. 'The Concepts of Obligation and Duty.' *Mind* 73 (1964).

Brandt, Richard. 'Traits of Character: A Conceptual Analysis.' *American Philosophical Quarterly* 7 (1970).

Brandt, Richard and Kim, Jaegwon. 'Wants as Explanations of Actions.' *Journal of Philosophy* 60 (1963).

Broad, C. D. *Five Types of Ethical Theory.* London: Oxford University Press, 1930.

Burnyeat, Myles. 'Virtues in Action.' *The Philosophy of Socrates.* Edited by G. Vlastos. Garden City, N.Y.: Doubleday, 1971.

Butler, Joseph. *Five Sermons.* Indianapolis: Bobbs-Merrill, 1950 reprint of 1726 edn.

Cant, Ronald. 'Origins of the Enlightenment in Scotland: the Universities.' In R. H. Campbell and Andrew Skinner, *The Origins and Nature of the Scottish Enlightenment.* Edinburgh: John Donald Publishers, 1982.

Capron, Alexander. 'Informed Consent in Catastrophic Disease Research and Treatment.' *University of Pennsylvania Law Review* 123 (1974).

Chappell, Vere. *Hume.* South Bend, Ind.: University of Notre Dame Press, 1966.

Bibliography

Childress, James. *Who Should Decide?: Paternalism in Health Care*. New York: Oxford University Press, 1982.

Chisholm, Roderick. 'Supererogation and Offence: A Conceptual Scheme for Ethics.' *Ratio* 5 (1963).

Churchland, Paul. 'The Logical Character of Action Explanations.' *Philosophical Review* 79 (1970).

Cicero, Marcus Tullius. *De Officiis*. Translated by T. Cockman Duncan. London: Routledge, 1894.

Cicero, Marcus Tullius. *De Republica*. Translated by G. Sabine and S. Smith. Indianapolis: Bobbs-Merrill, 1929.

Cooper, Anthony (Lord Shaftesbury). *Characteristics of Men, Manners, Opinions, Times*. Indianapolis: Bobbs-Merrill, 1964 reprint of 1711 edn.

Cranor, Carl. 'Toward a Theory of Respect for Persons.'' *American Philosophical Quarterly* 12 (1975).

Culver, Charles and Gert, Bernard. *Philosophy in Medicine: Conceptual and Ethical Issues in Medicine and Psychiatry*. New York: Oxford University Press, 1982.

Darwall, Stephen. 'Two Kinds of Respect.' *Ethics* 88 (1977).

Darwall, Stephen. 'Practical Skepticism and the Reasons for Action.' *Canadian Journal of Philosophy* 8 (1978).

Darwall, Stephen. 'Is There a Kantian Foundation for Rawlsian Justice?' *John Rawls' Theory of Social Justice*. Edited by H. Blocker and E. Smith. Athens: Ohio University Press, 1980.

Darwall, Stephen. *Impartial Reason*. Ithaca: Cornell University Press, 1983.

d'Entreves, A. P. *Aquinas: Selected Political Writings*. Oxford: Oxford University Press, 1948.

d'Entreves, A. P. *Natural Law: An Introduction to Legal Philosophy*. London: Hutchinson's University Library, 1951.

Descartes, René. *Oeuvres de Descartes*. Edited by Charles Adam and Paul Tannery. Paris, 1913.

Descartes, René. *The Philosophical Works of Descartes*. Translated by E. S. Haldane and G. R. T. Ross. 2 vols. Cambridge: Cambridge University Press, 1967.

Donagan, Alan. *The Theory of Morality*. Chicago: University of Chicago Press, 1977.

Donagan, Alan. 'Consistency in Rationalist Moral Systems.' *Journal of Philosophy* 81 (1984).

Downie, R. S. and Telfer, Elizabeth. *Respect for Persons*. London: George Allen & Unwin, 1969.

Eisenberg, Paul. 'From the Forbidden to the Supererogatory: The Basic Ethical Categories in Kant's *Tugendlehre*.' *American Philosophical Quarterly* 3 (1966).

Emerson, R. L. 'Scottish Universities in the Eighteenth Century, 1690–1800.' *Studies in Voltaire and the Eighteenth Century* 167 (1977).

Falk, W. D. 'Hume on Practical Reason.' *Philosophical Studies* 27 (1975).

Falk, W. D. 'Hume on Is and Ought.' *Canadian Journal of Philosophy* 6 (1976).

Bibliography

Feinberg, Joel. 'Supererogation and Rules.' *International Journal of Ethics* 71 (1961).

Fellner, C. H. and Marshall, J. R. 'Kidney Donors: The Myth of Informed Consent.' *American Journal of Psychiatry* 126 (1970).

Forbes, Duncan. *Hume's Philosophical Politics*. Cambridge: Cambridge University Press, 1975.

Forbes, Duncan. 'Natural Law and the Scottish Enlightenment.' In R. H. Campbell and Andrew Skinner, *The Origins and Nature of the Scottish Enlightenment*. Edinburgh: John Donald Publishers, 1982.

Frankena, William. 'Pritchard and the Ethics of Virtue.' *The Monist* 54 (1970).

Frankena, William. *Ethics*. Englewood Cliffs, N.J.: Prentice-Hall, 1973.

Green, O. H. (ed.). *Respect for Persons*. New Orleans: Tulane University, 1982.

Harrison, Jonathan. 'The Expedient, the Right, and the Just in Mill's *Utilitarianism*.' *Canadian Journal of Philosophy, Supplementary Volume* 1 (1974).

Hart, H. L. A. 'Are There Any Natural Rights?' *Philosophical Review* 64 (1955).

Hempel, Carl. 'Logical Positivism and the Social Sciences.' *The Legacy of Logical Positivism*. Edited by P. Achinstein and S. Barker. Baltimore: Johns Hopkins Press, 1969.

Hill, Thomas E., Jr. 'Kant on Imperfect Duty and Supererogation.' *Kant-Studien* 62 (1971).

Hill, Thomas E., Jr. 'Servility and Self-Respect.' *The Monist* 57 (1973).

Hudson, Stephen. 'Character Traits and Desires.' *Ethics* 90 (1980).

Hudson, Stephen. 'The Nature of Respect.' *Social Theory and Practice* 6 (1980).

Hudson, Stephen. 'Taking Virtues Seriously.' *Australasian Journal of Philosophy* 59 (1981).

Hudson, Stephen. 'Right Reason and Mortal Gods.' *The Monist* 66 (1983).

Hume, David. *The Letters of David Hume*. Edited by J. Y. T. Greig. 2 vols. Oxford: Clarendon Press, 1932.

Hume, David. *An Abstract of A Treatise of Human Nature 1740*. London: Cambridge University Press, 1938 reprint.

Hume, David. *An Inquiry Concerning the Principles of Morals*. Edited by Charles W. Hendel. Indianapolis: Bobbs-Merrill, 1957 reprint of 1751 edn.

Hume, David. *David Hume: The Philosophical Works*. Edited by T. H. Green and T. H. Grose. 4 vols. Darmstadt: Scientia Verlag Aalen, 1964 reprint of 1886 edn.

Hume, David. *A Treatise of Human Nature*. Edited by L. A. Selby-Bigge. London: Oxford University Press, 1968 reprint of the 1888 edn.

Hume, David. *The History of Great Britain: The Reign of James I and Charles I*. Harmondsworth: Penguin Books, 1970.

Hume, David. *Enquiries Concerning Human Understanding and Concerning the Principles of Morals*. Edited by L. A. Selby-Bigge. London: Oxford University Press, 1975.

Bibliography

Hutcheson, Francis. *An Inquiry into the Original of our Ideas of Beauty and Virtue*. Farnborough: Gregg International Publishers, 1969 reprint of the fourth edn. of 1738.

Ingelfinger, Franz. 'Arrogance.' *New England Journal of Medicine* 303 (1980).

Jones, Peter. 'Cause, Reason, and Objectivity in Hume's Aesthetics.' *Hume: A Re-evaluation*. Edited by J.T. King and D. Livingston. New York: Fordham University Press, 1976.

Kant, Immanuel. *Critique of Practical Reason*. Translated by L.W. Beck. Indianapolis: Bobbs-Merrill, 1956 reprint of 1788 edn.

Kant, Immanuel. *Foundations of the Metaphysics of Morals*. Translated by L.W. Beck. Indianapolis: Bobbs-Merrill, 1959 reprint of 1785 edn.

Kant, Immanuel. *The Metaphysical Elements of Justice: Part I of The Metaphysics of Morals*. Translated by John Ladd. Indianapolis: Bobbs-Merrill, 1965 reprint of 1797 edn.

Kenny, Anthony. 'Descartes on Ideas.' *Descartes: A Collection of Critical Essays*. Edited by Willis Doney. Garden City, N.Y.: Doubleday, 1967.

King, J.T. 'The Place of the Language of Morals in Hume's Second Enquiry.' *Hume: A Re-evaluation*. Edited by J.T. King and D. Livingston. New York: Fordham University Press, 1976.

Lawrence, Roy. *Motive and Intention*. Evanston: Northwestern University Press, 1972.

Lyons, David. 'Human Rights and the General Welfare.' *Philosophy and Public Affairs* 6 (1977).

Macfie, A.L. 'The Scottish Tradition in Economic Thought.' *The Individual in Society: Essays on Adam Smith*. London: Allen & Unwin, 1967.

MacIntyre, Alasdair. 'Hume on "Is" and "Ought".' In V. Chappell, *Hume*. South Bend, Ind.: University of Notre Dame Press, 1966.

MacIntyre, Alasdair. *After Virtue*. Notre Dame, Ind.: University of Notre Dame Press, 1981.

Marcus, Ruth Barcan. 'Moral Dilemmas and Consistency.' *Journal of Philosophy* 78 (1980).

Martineau, James. *Types of Ethical Theory*, 2 vols, 1885.

Mill, John Stuart. *Utilitarianism*. Indianapolis: Bobbs-Merrill, 1971 reprint of 1864 edn.

Moore, James and Silverthorne, Michael. 'Gershom Carmichael and the Natural Jurisprudence Tradition in Eighteenth Century Scotland.' In Roger Emerson (ed.), *Man and Nature*. London, Ontario: University of Western Ontario, 1982.

Moore, James and Silverthorne, Michael. 'Natural Sociability and Natural Rights in the Moral Philosophy of Gerschom Carmichael.' In V. Hope (ed.), *Philosophers of the Scottish Enlightenment*. Edinburgh: Edinburgh University Press, 1984.

Morris, Herbert. 'Persons and Punishment.' *The Monist* 52 (1968).

Murdoch, Iris. *The Sovereignty of Good*. New York: Schocken, 1971.

Norton, David F. *David Hume: Common-Sense Moralist, Sceptical Metaphysician*. Princeton: Princeton University Press, 1982.

Nussbaum, Martha. 'Shame, Separateness, and Political Unity: Aris-

Bibliography

totle's Criticism of Plato.' *Essays on Aristotle's Ethics*. Edited by A. O. Rorty. Berkeley: University of California Press, 1980.

Penner, Terry. 'The Unity of Virtue.' *Philosophical Review* 82 (1973).

Pope, Alexander. *Essay on Man*. Edited by Frank Brady. Indianapolis: Bobbs-Merrill, 1965.

Price, Richard. *A Review of the Principal Questions in Morals*. Edited by D. D. Raphael. London: Oxford University Press, 1948 reprint of 3rd edn, 1787.

Prior, A. N. 'The Virtue of the Act and the Virtue of the Agent.' *Philosophy* 26 (1951).

Pufendorf, Samuel. *De Jure Naturae Et Gentium Libri Octo*. tr. Oldfather and Oldfather. Oxford: Clarendon Press, 1934 reprint of 1688 edn.

Raphael, D. D. *The Moral Sense*. London: Oxford University Press, 1947.

Raphael, D. D. 'The Impartial Spectator.' *Proceedings of the British Academy* 58 (1972).

Rawls, John. 'Two Concepts of Rules.' *Philosophical Review* 64 (1955).

Rawls, John. *A Theory of Justice*. Cambridge, Mass: Harvard University Press, 1971.

Reid, Thomas. *Essays on the Active Powers of the Human Mind*. Cambridge, Mass: M.I.T. Press, 1969 reprint of 1788 edn.

Robison, Wade L. and Pritchard, Michael S. (eds). *Medical Responsibility: Paternalism, Informed Consent, and Euthanasia*. Clifton, N.J.: Humana Press, 1979.

Ross, W. D. *The Right and the Good*. London: Oxford University Press, 1930.

Ross, W. D. *Foundations of Ethics*. London: Oxford University Press, 1939.

Rousseau, Jean-Jacques. *The First and Second Discourses*. Translated by Roger D. and Judith R. Masters. New York: St Martin's Press, 1964.

Sachs, David. 'How to Distinguish Self-Respect from Self-Esteem.' *Philosophy and Public Affairs* 19 (1981).

Schneewind, J. B. *Sidgwick's Ethics and Victorian Moral Philosophy*. London: Oxford University Press, 1977.

Shelp, Earl. *Beneficence and Health Care*. Dordrecht, Holland: D. Reidel Publishing Co., 1982.

Sidgwick, Henry. *The Methods of Ethics*. Chicago: University of Chicago Press, 1962 reprint of seventh edn.

Smith, Norman Kemp. *The Philosophy of David Hume*. New York: St Martin's Press, 1966.

Stein, Peter. 'The Influence of Roman Law on the Law of Scotland.' *The Juridical Review* 8 N.S. (1963).

Urmson, J. O. 'Saints and Heroes.' *Essays in Moral Philosophy*. Edited by A. I. Melden. Seattle: University of Washington Press, 1958.

von Wright, G. H. *The Varieties of Goodness*. London: Routledge & Kegan Paul, 1963.

Wallace, James. 'Excellences and Merit.' *Philosophical Review* 83 (1974).

Whiteley, C. H. 'On Duties.' *Proceedings of the Aristotelian Society* 53 (1952-3).

Bibliography

Williams, Bernard. 'Ethical Consistency.' *Problems of the Self*. New York: Cambridge University Press, 1977.

Williams, Bernard. 'Persons, Character and Morality.' *Moral Luck*. Cambridge: Cambridge University Press, 1981.

Zeller, Eduard. *The Stoics, Epicureans and Sceptics*. London: Longmans, Green & Co., 1892.

Index

Index

Index

ethics of duty, 36–8
ethics of virtues, 36–8
exhibiting a virtue, 45–50
expectations, 76–7, 138–9

Falk, W.D., 136
Feinberg, Joel, 125
Fellner, C.H., 150
final cause, 88–90
Forbes, Duncan, 148
formal goodness, 52
Frankena, William, 36–8, 124
friendship, 33–5, 62, 98–9, 101–2
functions, 11–12, 24–5

Gert, Bernard, 150
Grotius, Hugo, 32, 103

habits, 76–7, 143
Harrison, Jonathan, 125
Hart, H.L.A., 125
Hempel, Carl, 128
Hill, Thomas, E., Jr, 126, 132
Hobbes, Thomas, 25, 73, 76, 84, 94, 97, 99, 101, 115
Hume, David, 4, 32–3, 59–60; on the Judicious Critic, 69, 72, 78, 91–4, 136; natural and artificial virtues, 73–88, 139–40; objects of moral judgement, 63, 69–70, 76, 79–81, 137; origin of morals, 63, 66–9, 74, 143; principles, 66–8, 143; self-respect and character, 61, 63–6, 99–100, 108, 133–5; sympathy, 61, 74–8, 87–8, 96, 135, 138, 144–5; theory of taste, 69
Hutcheson, Francis, 66, 89, 103, 137, 140, 148

identification, 65–6, 74–7, 120–2
impartiality, 84–6, 90–1, 94, 111–12
imperfect duties, 31–3, 102, 126
impersonal point of view, 25, 84–6, 93, 95–7, 115–17
Indirect View, 4–7, 37–50, 106–8, 149; strong and weak denial, 6

individualism, 76, 120
Ingelfinger, Franz, 150
intentions: and motives, 48–9, 53–60; Price's account, 54–7
intercourse of sentiments, 75–6, 138
intuitionist theory, 8

Jones, Peter, 136
Judicious Critic, 69, 72, 78, 91–4, 136

Kant, Immanuel, 4, 6, 10, 25–6, 30, 31–2, 40, 57, 85, 94–5, 106–7, 113–14, 126; Indirect View, 4, 57, 123, 149; reason and transcendental freedom, 56–7, 96, 114–15, 145, 149; and the social contract, 101–2, 118–22; veil of ignorance, 95, 120–2
Kenny, Anthony, 131
Kim, Jaegwon, 128
King, J.T., 136
Kingdom of Ends, 102, 110, 150–1
Kingdom of God, 150–1

Lawrence, Roy, 130
liberalism, 4, 8, 111
Locke, John, 25, 66, 76, 89, 101
Logos, 114
Lyons, David, 125

Macfie, A.L., 147
MacIntyre, Alasdair, 125, 143
Mandeville, Bernard, 66, 99, 135, 140
Marcus, Ruth, 142
Marshall, James, 150
Martineau, James, 6, 40, 47–50, 123
material goodness, 52
megalopsuchos, 64
metamoral, 2–4, 7–8, 90–1, 151
Mill, John Stuart, 30–1, 51, 58–60, 125
minimalist morality, 33
Moore, G.E., 10